BELL'S CATHEDRALS:
THE CATHEDRAL CHURCH
OF CHICHESTER

LECTOR HOUSE PUBLIC DOMAIN WORKS

BELL'S CATHEDRALS:
THE CATHEDRAL CHURCH OF CHICHESTER

HUBERT CHRISTIAN CORLETTE

ISBN: 978-93-89701-46-3

Published: 1901

© 2020
LECTOR HOUSE LLP

LECTOR HOUSE LLP
E-MAIL: lectorpublishing@gmail.com

CHICHESTER CATHEDRAL FROM THE SOUTH.

BELL'S CATHEDRALS:
THE CATHEDRAL CHURCH
OF CHICHESTER

A SHORT HISTORY & DESCRIPTION OF ITS FABRIC WITH AN ACCOUNT OF THE DIOCESE AND SEE

BY

HUBERT C. CORLETTE

A.R.I.B.A.

ARMS OF THE SEE.

WITH XLV ILLUSTRATIONS

1901

PREFACE.

All the facts of the following history were supplied to me by many authorities. To a number of these, references are given in the text. But I wish to acknowledge how much I owe to the very careful and original research provided by Professor Willis, in his "Architectural History of the Cathedral"; by Precentor Walcott, in his "Early Statutes" of Chichester; and Dean Stephen, in his "Diocesan History." The footnotes, which refer to the latter work, indicate the pages in the smaller edition. But the volume could never have been completed without the great help given to me on many occassions by Prebendary Bennett. His deep and intimate knowledge of the cathedral structure and its history was always at my disposal. It is to him, as well as to Dr. Codrington and Mr. Gordon P.G. Hills, I am still further indebted for much help in correcting the proofs and for many valuable suggestions.

H.C.C.

CONTENTS

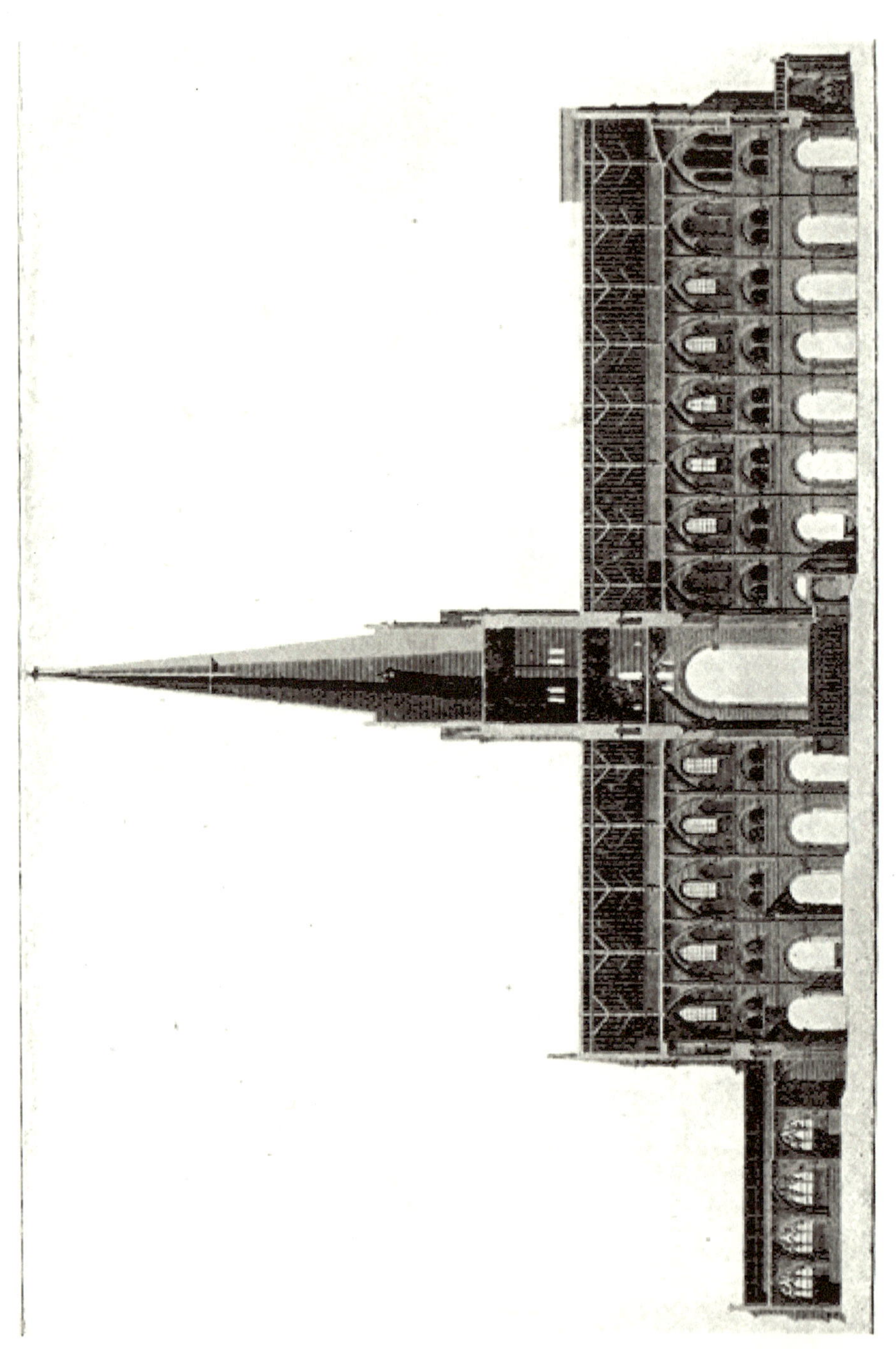

LONGITUDINAL SECTION, ABOUT 1815 SHOWING THE ARUN-DEL SCREEN AND THE POSITION OF THE REREDOS.

From Dallaway's "West Sussex." (scale 75 feet to 1 in.)

CHICHESTER CATHEDRAL FROM THE EAST.

CHAPTER I.

THE HISTORY OF THE CATHEDRAL.

Any attempt to write the history of a cathedral requires that the subject shall be approached with two leading ideas in view. One of these has reference to the history of a Church; the other to the story of a building. The two aspects are clearly to be distinguished, but their mutual relation may be better appreciated when we realise how intimately they are bound together.

Ecclesiastical history, or "ecclesiology," and architectural history, or "archae-ology," do not exist apart; for the needs of Christian liturgy indicated what ar-rangement was required in those buildings that were peculiarly dedicated to the use of the Church; hence we have, in the mere building itself, to consider the con-dition of ecclesiastical and architectural growth displayed by its character during each stage of its development, and this development, this character, is to be dis-covered as well in the plan and structure of the fabric, with its decorative details, as in the record that documents and traditions have preserved. But we need to remember that one see, one building, represents a link in one long continuing chain, and in doing this we naturally look back as well as forward to observe the relation of either to the past and to the present. Such an attitude as this requires that we refer to that period when the subject of this chapter was not yet part of the native soil of Sussex, and in doing this we find that so early as the eighth century the town of Chichester was even then a known centre of civil, though apparently not ecclesiastical, activity; for it is not until about the middle of the tenth century that some uncertain documentary evidence refers to "Bishop Brethelm and the brethren dwelling at Chichester."[1] It may be that Brethelm was a bishop in, though not of, Chichester, who dwelt and worked among the south Saxons living in and about the city, for the history of the diocese and see will show that probably there was no episcopate established under that name until a little more than one hundred years later.

Ceadwalla's foundation of the see at Selsea dated from about the end of the seventh century; but we know nothing about any cathedral church at that place during the following three hundred and fifty years. If, however, there was a bishop in charge of the missionary priests, deacons, and laymen who lived there together, there must necessarily have been a "cathedra" in the church they used.

When Stigand came from Selsea to establish his see in Chichester he found the city already furnished with a minster dedicated to S. Peter. He had effected this transfer because the Council of London had decided in 1075 that all the then village sees should be removed to towns; and as there is no evidence of any attempt to provide a new cathedral until about the year 1088, the existing minster must have been appropriated for the see. It has been supposed that Stigand may have devised some scheme for building a new church, and even that he saw it carried out so far as to provide the foundations on which to execute this idea. But there appears to be no authority which warrants the assumption that he did even so much as this, for history says nothing about such an early beginning of the new operations, tradition asserts no more, and speculation suggests probabilities merely. We are obliged, therefore, to be satisfied with the fact that the work begun about 1088 was consecrated by Bishop Ralph de Luffa, in 1108, and it is possible even now to see the stone which commemorates that ceremony embedded in the walling of the present church. Unfortunately no more than about six years had passed since this, the first, dedication, when a fire occurred which burnt part of the fabric. Ralph was still living, and began at once to repair the damage that had been done; and the king (Henry I.) gave him much help by encouraging his endeavour. What, then, had been accomplished during the twenty years between 1088 and 1108?

In 1075 Stigand transferred the see. About thirteen years later the new cathedral building appears to have been begun under Ralph, and in another twenty years so much had been finished as would allow him to see it dedicated. It is probable that before this ceremony was performed a considerable portion of the eastern section of the work was finished; for in accordance with a general custom with the mediæval church builders, this part would have been that first begun. But how much of it was ready for use? The sanctuary and presbytery, or choir, with its necessary structural appendages, no doubt first appeared. It may be that no more

[1] Walcott, "Early Statutes," p. 12.

than this was ready when the dedication took place. But it is not possible to say with any authority what actually was finished. Nevertheless, the character of the building itself explains the course in which the structure was developed. After the first fire, in 1114, the work steadily continued, and it is possible that before that mishap occurred, certain other parts had been begun, if not finished. The remains of the original nave still present distinct evidence to show that it was, with the aisles, built in two sections; and these, although they appear at first to be alike, prove upon closer examination that the four bays towards the west are of a later date than those other four eastward. Now it is not essential that we should know exactly how much of the building was finished by a certain year, or what stage towards completion had been reached at any particular time; it is sufficient at present that we should be able to indicate the general trend of the operations,—and this would suggest the conclusion that, having prepared so much as was necessary about the chancel, the builders went on busily, after the dedication, to deal with the transept and the nave. Then followed those four early bays of the nave which are nearest to the east.

It is quite safe to assume upon various grounds that the work had been carried on successfully up to this stage early in the twelfth century; but neither the documentary evidence available, nor the condition of the fabric, enables us to venture more than this surmise concerning its condition at that time.

Between 1114 and the time of the second and serious fire in 1187, the remainder of the whole scheme planned a hundred years before was apparently finished.

The first fire had excited some public interest in the great enterprise at Chichester, and from this an impetus was derived which helped towards its execution, after the small damage caused by the fire had been quickly repaired, for by about the year 1150 the four western bays of the nave, with its aisles, must have been complete. It should be understood that the fire in 1114 did not lead to any change in the character of the church such as was occasioned by that other fire which shall be considered presently; but the work had quietly continued, so that the aisles of the nave were vaulted by about 1170-1180, the lady-chapel was completed, and in 1184 all was ready for the second ceremony of consecration which then took place. It has been assumed that this act implies that the whole of the original scheme had been executed. Nevertheless, it must be acknowledged that again there are but few authentic records to show in what manner the work had been carried on, nor are there many indications of the way in which the necessary materials and money were provided to help it forward. But it is interesting to notice that in 1147 William, Earl of Arundel, gave to the see that quarter of the city in which stood the palace of the bishops, the residences of the canons, and the cathedral church. This grant of land confirmed the see in its possession of all that part of the city now within the bounds of the close.

From Winkle's Cathedrals.

THE WEST FRONT, ABOUT 1836.

What, then, was the plan of that church which was designed to suit the requirements set down by Bishop Ralph Luffa? The ground-plan at the end of the volume shows the building as it now remains, after many alterations have been made in the original scheme; but the arrangement is still, in its main features, much the same as was at first devised. The usual plan was adopted, and this was the provision of a nave and chancel having a transept between them so as to make the form of a cross. The nave had aisles along its whole length. These were extended on both sides eastward of the transept, and continued as an ambulatory round a semicircular apse. The transept also had a small apsidal chapel on the east side of both its north and south arms. At the point of intersection between the transept and the nave the supports of the central tower rose. Between this and the west end there were eight arches in each of the arcades opening north and south from the nave into the aisles. Beyond the crossing towards the east there were three similar arches in the arcades which connected the apse with the large piers of the central tower. These three bays, together with the apse, enclosed the chancel; and this comprised the sanctuary, which was that part within the apse itself, and also the presbytery, or choir of the priests, which occupied the remaining space between the apse and the arch into the transept beneath the tower. At a later date the accommodation of the choir was increased by making it occupy part of the space farther to the west. Possibly it projected into the nave. At the west end of each of the aisles of the nave a tower was placed, and between these two towers was the chief public entrance to the church. From the subsequent history of the structure it would appear that the two western towers had been built up and finished, so far, at least, as was necessary to allow of the completion of the nave with its aisles and roofs. The same may be concluded of the central tower.

This latter probably rose only just above the ridge of the roofs. To carry it up so far would have been dictated to the builders by structural reasons; for such a height would be required to help the stability of the piers and arches below, since they had to resist a variety of opposed thrusts. But even this tower, low as it no doubt was, like others of the same date, did not survive the dedication more than about twenty-six years. The whole building was covered with a high-pitched wooden roof over the nave, transept, and chancel; and beneath the outer roof there was a flat inner ceiling of wood formed between the tie beams, similar to those now to be seen at Peterborough and S. Albans. The north and south aisles of the nave were protected by roofs which sloped up from their eaves against the wall that rose above the nave arcades. Internally the ceiling to these was a simple groined vault supported by transverse arches.

Immediately above the vault of the aisles was the gallery of the triforium. This was lighted throughout by small external round-headed windows, some of which may still be seen embedded in the walls. The aisles and ambulatory of the chancel were treated by the same methods. In the triforium gallery, above the transverse arches of the aisles, were other semicircular arches. These served a double purpose: they acted as supports to the timber framework of the aisle roofs, and also as a means of buttressing the upper part of the nave walling in which the clerestory windows were placed. Such other buttresses as there had been were broad and

flat, with but little projection from the surface of the wall. The windows throughout the building up to about the end of the twelfth century were small in comparison with some of those which were inserted at various times afterwards.

From a photograph by Mr. F. Bond.

VIEW THROUGH THE SOUTH TRIFORIUM OF THE NAVE FROM THE SOUTH-WEST TOWER.

It has been remarked that the termination of the early chancel towards the east
was an apse, and that round this was carried the north and south choir aisles in the
form of a continuous ambulatory. From this enclosing aisle—a semi-circle itself in
form—three chapels were projected, each with a semicircular apsidal termination.
The central one of the three was the lady-chapel. This consisted then of the three
western bays only of the present chapel. The lady-chapel was added about eighty
years after the early part of the nave had been built, and has since been much al-

tered.

The presence of this grouping of features is indicative of that influence which Continental architecture had exercised upon English art, and now that Norman government had been established that influence became more directly French. But though so strongly affected by this means, Anglo-Saxon character was always evident in work which was a native expression of the thought and personality of those by whom it was executed.

Thus we see that the plan which Ralph approved for the new church that was to be built for him at Chichester was devised according to accepted traditional arrangement. He adopted no new idea when he decided what general form the cathedral should follow. The disposition of the several parts differed in no wise from that which had been followed during centuries before. The requirements of ritual had decided long since what were those essential features of planning to be insisted upon, for the pattern in germ was shown in the arrangement of the Mosaic Tabernacle. In the earliest plans the same distribution of parts was observed, though at a later date the transept was introduced—an idea which no doubt had its origin in some practical necessity, and was afterwards retained as being representative of an ecclesiastical symbol.

Of the practical and artistic character of the architectural details we shall see more in examining the exterior and the interior of the church. These will lead us, of necessity, to deal more with archaeology in its relation to the history of architecture rather than of this particular church as a building used for ecclesiastical purposes.

After the ceremony of 1184 building operations were continued, but the records available do not tell about anything of much interest for the next two or three years. Then in 1186-1187 a catastrophe occurred—the cathedral was again burnt. But this time the effects of the fire were much more disastrous than had been the case in 1114. So extensive was the destruction that the entire roofing, as well as the internal flat ceiling, was gone; and though we can glean no certain knowledge from documentary evidence, it appears probable that the eastern section of the building suffered more than any other, for whatever other causes may have aided in the wreck of this part—a weakness in the masonry, an insufficiency in the supports or abutments—the fall of such heavy timbers as those which must have formed the outer roof and inner ceiling of the chancel would in itself be sufficient to wreck the remainder.

Whether the change in plan that now followed was really necessary because of the damage that had been done, or whether the fire provided a welcome opportunity by which new features might be introduced, we are not able to discover. It is sufficient that the chance was not lost, for in the eastern ambulatory of the cathedral church at Chichester is to be seen, as a result, one of the most truly beautiful examples of mediæval design that English architecture now possesses.

From a photograph by Mr. F. Bond.

THE CLERESTORY PASSAGE, NAVE, SOUTH SIDE.

In the nave some parts of the old limestone walls had been injured by the fall of the roofs; they were also seriously damaged by the beams that had been laid upon them, for these, after their fall, would continue to burn as they rested against those portions of walling which remained standing. It was no doubt by some such cause as this that the early clerestory was disfigured and partly destroyed. In either case, the old clerestory arcade of the twelfth century no longer remained as it was before; and though there were already stone vaults to the aisles of the nave before the fire occurred, yet they also disappeared and made way for newer ones.

The outer roof over the triforium evidently shared the fate of the other coverings; and the arched abutment in the triforium, which acted as a support to this roof and the walling below the clerestory, now disappeared. It may be that this arching was not completely destroyed by the fire alone; no doubt some that remained was intentionally removed to prepare the way for the new work.

The same bishop who had witnessed the completion of the earlier operations began with much enterprise to see about the reconstruction, but not the restoration, of what had been destroyed. Some portions were repaired, others rebuilt; but the greater part of the work now undertaken involved an entire change in the character of some of the principal features of the earlier scheme. In fact, this incident in the history of our subject gave "occasion to one of the most curious and interesting examples of the methods employed by the mediæval architects in the repairs of their buildings."[2]

Having decided that they would, if possible, avoid all future risk of a similar catastrophe, a system of vaulting was adopted as the best solution of the problem, — this involved necessarily a remodelling of the interior; and so, neglecting the Isle of Wight limestone and the Sussex sandstone, which at first had been the material used for the walling, the masons were directed to use stone of finer texture and smaller grain. It has been thought by some that this material was brought from Caen in Normandy. The same stone was used to re-face parts of the nave piers. And in addition Purbeck marble was selected instead of that which was to be found in Sussex.

It is interesting to remember that the new choir of Canterbury had only been finished about three years before the fire occurred at Chichester. This work had been begun by William of Sens and finished by William the Englishman; and though it was so large an undertaking, it appears to have been commenced and completed between the years 1174 and 1184. This would very naturally exert some influence upon the building projects of a neighbouring see. Whether any of the actual craftsmen from Canterbury worked again at Chichester or not we cannot tell, but it is evident that the Kentish experience was of great help to Sussex in the new venture. When it had been decided how they should operate, it was natural that the covering of the building must be the first provision. This involved the repair of the shattered clerestory, and then they were free to proceed in other directions. Further than this we have no means of learning what method was followed in carrying on the new work; but it continued, so that in about twelve years the building was dedicated again.

---

[2] Willis, "Chichester Cathedral," p. 6.

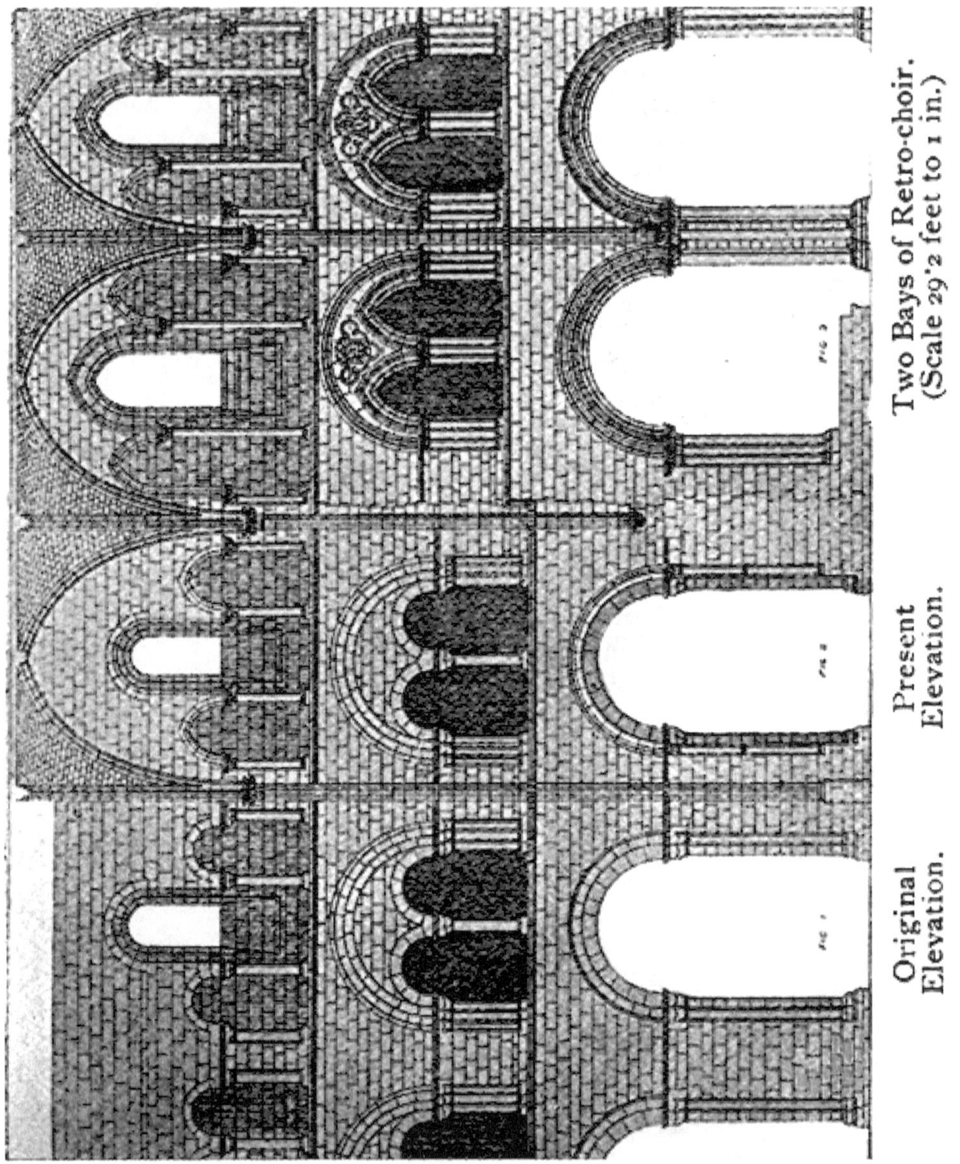

**HISTORICAL SECTION FROM WILLIS'S ARCHITECTURAL HIS-
TORY.**

There is nothing now to indicate that the provision of a vault had been intended by the original builders of these walls. This deficiency was met by the insertion
of vaulting shafts and the addition of external buttressing; for as the pressure of
the flat wooden roof was exerted for the most part vertically upon its supports,
that of the vault would be a strong lateral thrust as well as vertical pressure, and
these were to be provided for. We shall see presently that all the real beauties of

this most interesting work were the outcome both of the needs of practical structure and the requirements of ritual and a ceremonial expression of the liturgy.

From a photograph by Mr. Francis Bond.

THE CLERESTORY, NORTH SIDE OF NAVE.

It is not possible for us to discover exactly when the several parts of the work
undertaken after the fire of 1186-1187 were begun, nor when they were finished.

Of dates we have little knowledge, except that of the dedication in 1199, the fall of two towers in 1210, and the various indications of architectural activity at certain periods given by the several dates mentioned in connection with donations, bequests, and royal sanctions in the episcopal statutes and other documents. These nearly all show that the time of greatest activity was after 1186 and before 1250. If such a feat as has been mentioned was performed at Canterbury between 1174 and 1184, was it not possible also at Chichester? Then it becomes necessary to assume that the structural alterations were continuing during the whole of the period suggested; and this was so. Enough work had been done by 1199 to allow of another dedication of the building. Seffrid II. had been bishop from 1180-1204, and the register of Bishop William Rede, written one hundred and sixty years later, explicitly states that Seffrid "re-edified the Church of Chichester." This is a comprehensive statement, but it might easily include at least the greater part of the vaulting with some form of external roof. Such a change as this involved the alteration of the nave and aisle piers, so that the slight vaulting shafts of finer stone might be inserted in the older masonry. The lower part of each of the piers of the nave arcade on the side towards the centre of the church was re-faced with the same material, and smaller shafts of Purbeck marble were introduced upon the piers, replacing probably the heavy ones of an earlier date. These shafts formed the support to a more delicate moulded member, which was now substituted for the original and very simple outer order of the original arch. A string-course of Purbeck marble was inserted as a line of separation between the nave arcade and the triforium, and also between the triforium and clerestory. The triforium itself remained as it had been before 1186; but the clerestory was dressed again, so that it obtained quite a new character. It was re-faced with the fine-grained stone, and the slight shafts which supported the clerestory arcades were provided with Purbeck capitals and bases. This arcading itself was also changed from its earlier type. The central arch was still made round in form, but those on either side of it were each pointed, and all were more finely moulded than before. Above this point rises the new stone vault, which is carried upon a framework of strong transverse and diagonal ribs. Between these the shell, or filling, which formed the surface of the vault, is of chalk, roughly cut and irregularly laid; above this was placed a thick coat of concrete.

Some flying-buttresses were built now in order to meet the thrust exerted by the new arched vault of the nave. These were constructed in two series, one being concealed under the sloping roof over the triforium and acting in place of the earlier round-arched abutment. Its supports were provided at the points where the transverse and diagonal arches of the nave vault began to spring away from the vertical plane of the walls. The other series was the immediate counter-poise to any direct thrust exerted by the arching of the vault against the upper section of the same walls. There was, in fact, a large buttress added to support these nave walls at that point from which each set of vault-carrying ribs began to rise. This buttress, though apparently sub-divided, was one thing, but of composite structure. It was pierced first by the aisle, next by the triforium, and then again above the roof of the triforium. It will be seen that most of these alterations were the direct result of the introduction of a stone vault. But the almost entire renewal of the eastern part of the cathedral was made possible by the destruction and total removal of the apsidal terminations of the earlier work. It has been suggested that the fire may have so badly damaged this portion as to allow no alternative but rebuilding. What may have been the actual cause of its removal it is impossible for us now to know; but the substitute is quite a perfect piece of work of its kind. This ambulatory, or presbytery, as it is commonly misnamed, was nearly all newly built from the foundations during the first half of the thirteenth century. The continuation of the arcade, the triforium, the clerestory, and the vault, the vaulting of the aisles and the chapels forming their terminations eastwards, — all this, with the new arch at the entrance to the earlier lady-chapel, was work of the same date.

From a photograph by S. B. Bolas & Co.

PIER-CAPITALS IN THE RETRO-CHOIR.

Some new buttressing had been added to the south-west tower when the upper part of the tower itself was rebuilt; but the larger works were the addition of a vaulted sacristy in the corner between the west side of the south end of the transept and the nave. On the opposite side of the same part of the transept a square-ended chapel with a vestry attached was added in place of the original shallow apsidal chapel. The original chapel on the east side of the north end of the transept was also removed to make way for another and much larger one. This is now used as the cathedral library.

The scheme planned after the second fire having been completed by about the middle of the thirteenth century, little further work was undertaken in comparison with that then finished; but before 1250 the wall of the south aisle of the nave was pierced in four bays, and two more chapels were added. Then, on the north of the nave, the outer wall of the aisle was cut through in the second bay, going west from the transept, and a small chapel was built. The other chapels west of this one were added during the latter half of the century. In each case the deeply projecting buttresses which had been introduced against the earlier walls after the second fire were used, where they were available, to form parts of the masonry of these new chapels, and were therefore not disturbed unnecessarily. The old walls having been altered, and the earlier buttresses being changed in their nature, it became necessary to carry the original thrust from the nave still farther out from its source in order to find for it some satisfactory abutment, and in doing this there was that new force, introduced by the vaulting of these added chapels, to be reckoned with in addition. Consequently, to the earlier buttressing more was added. The exact nature and the approximate date of this work are shown by Professor Willis in the sections and plan given in his monograph on the cathedral. The addition to each buttress amounted to an elongation of it as a pierced wing wall which provided lateral support. Upon the end of it a greater mass of masonry was introduced to serve as a weight for steadying the structural device; and this necessary structural idea was the means of introducing another architectural feature—the pinnacle. Between the pinnacles of these buttresses rose the gabled ends of each of the chapels. Professor Willis suggests that a great part of the work done after the fire of 1186-1187 was completed by the time of the dedication ceremony in 1199, and he is no doubt a safe authority to follow. But the nature of many architectural features tends very strongly to confirm the idea that much of the work in the ambulatory eastward of the sanctuary had been delayed. It may have been that the activity which prevailed during the early half of the thirteenth century was caused by the desire to see this portion of the church completed; and the energy with which the plea for new interest and further funds was urged at this time would no doubt be indicative of a supervening lethargy following on the great effort necessary for the completion of so much in these few years. But it should be remembered that these great works of mediæval art were none of them built in a day; they represented the accumulation of even centuries of developing thought and continually improving skill. Therefore must we realise that after this fire had occurred in 1186-1187 not more than eleven or twelve years elapsed before the building was again in use after the consecration in 1199.

Note.—For remarks on Chichester Cathedral, see Archaeologia, xvii., pp. 22-28: "Observations on the Origin of Gothic Architecture." By G. Saunders, 1814.

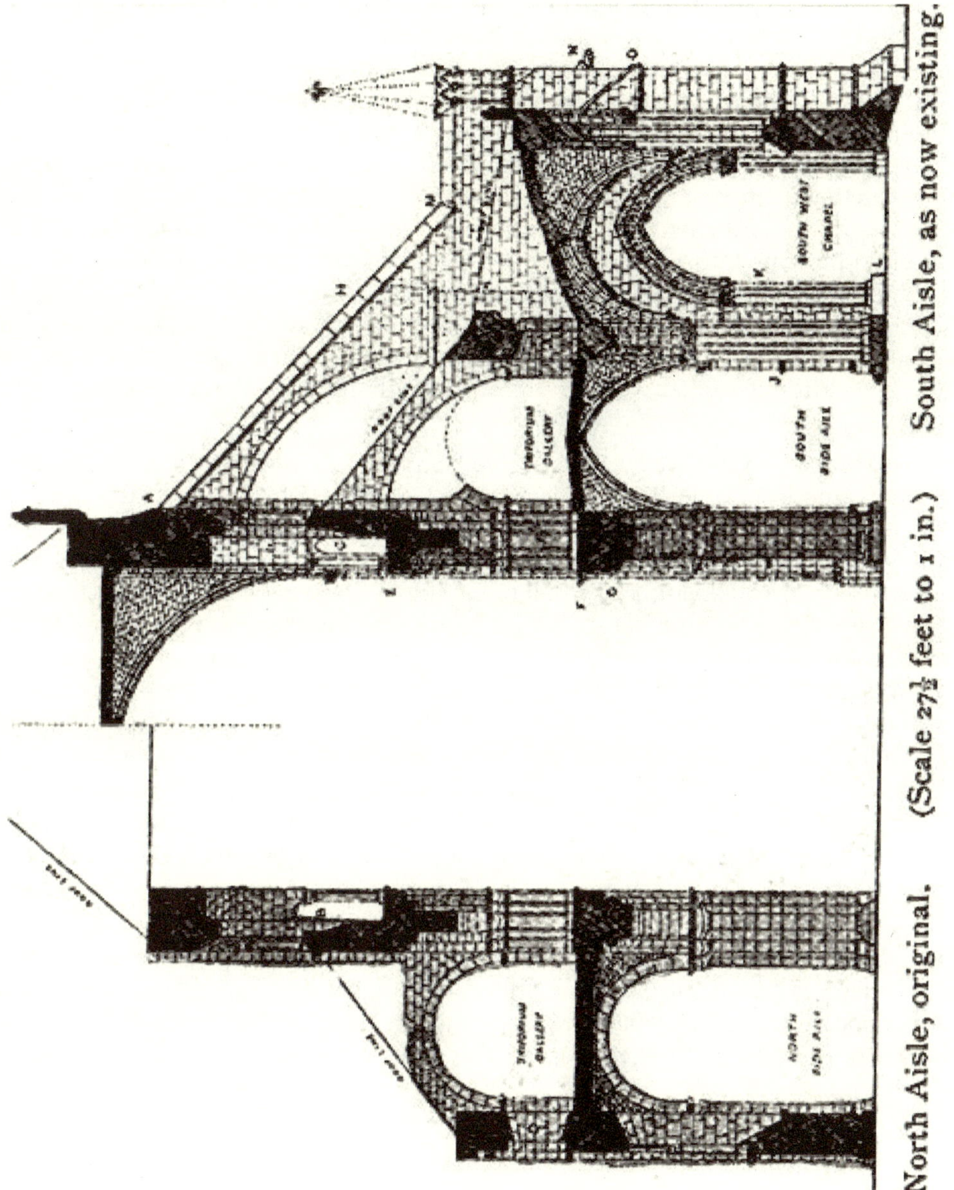

TRANSVERSE SECTIONS FROM WILLIS'S ARCHITECTURAL HISTORY.

This process of reconstruction shows that the mediæval builders did not restore in duplication of what had been lost. Where their work was destroyed they built anew and improved upon what had gone.

We need not suppose that this repair, renewal, and addition had all been completed when in 1199 Bishop Seffrid II. and six other bishops again consecrated the church. Doubtless only so much had been done as was necessary to enable the priests to officiate at an altar provided for the purpose and the congregation to assemble within the walls; for the work of building continued with a somewhat persistent manifestation of energy throughout the whole of the thirteenth century. Of this activity and enterprise there are many evidences in proof, both documentary and structural. The documentary evidence indicating the activity which prevailed after this date is sufficient to show at least that much was being done; but it does not often indicate in precise terms what is that particular portion of the building to which it primarily refers. Early in the thirteenth century (1207) the king gave Bishop Simon de Welles (1204-1207) his written permission to bring marble from Purbeck for the repair of his church at Chichester. He attached to this act of favour certain conditions which were to prevent any disposal of the material for other purposes.

John had also two years before given Bakechild Church to the "newly-dedicated" cathedral. Then Bishop Neville, or Ralph II. (1224-1244), at his death in 1244, "Dedit cxxx. marcas ad fabricam Ecclesiae et capellam suam integram cum multis ornamentis." Walcott adds that "his executors, besides releasing a debt of £60 due to him and spent on the bell tower, gave £140 to the fabric of the Church, receiving some benefit in return." This cannot be interpreted as referring to the isolated tower standing apart to the north of the west front; for, as we shall see, this was not erected until at least one hundred and fifty years later. In 1232 "the dean and chapter gave of their substance. During five years they devoted to the glory and beauty of the House of the Lord a twentieth part of the income of every dignity and prebend";[3] and then, again, ten years after the period covered by this act of the chapter the bishops of some other sees granted indulgences on behalf of the fabric of the church at Chichester. Bishop Richard of Wych (1245-1253) "Dedit ad opus Ecclesiae Circestrensis ecclesias de Stoghton et Alceston, et jus patronatûs ecclesiae de Mundlesham, et pensionem xl. s. in eadem."[4] To this he added a bequest of £40. He had revived in 1249 a statute of his predecessor, Simon de Welles, and extended "the capitular contribution to half the revenues of every prebend, whilst one moiety of a prebend vacant by death went to the fabric and the rest to the use of the canons." Other means were used to provide funds to continue the work.

But apart from these many indications of activity, the fabric as it stands to-day speaks very clearly of the amount of building that went on between 1200 and 1300. But it was not till 1288-1305 that Bishop Gilbert de S. Leophardo had added the two new bays of the lady-chapel eastward.

The fire was the direct cause of most of the work that was done. There was another, however; for eleven years after the re-dedication, two of the towers fell. It has been supposed by some that these must have been the early towers of the west front, both of which still preserve indications of having been begun during the twelfth century as part of the original building scheme. It is probable, for reasons

[3] Walcott, "Early Statutes," p. 15.
[4] Walcott, p. 15.

that will appear later, that the two towers of the west front did not collapse at the time of the second fire, although it would seem from the Chronicle of Dunstable that their stability may have been impaired in some measure, since the sole cause for this fall of towers is given in the words "impetu venti ceciderunt duae turres Cicestriae."[5] But if these towers had been affected, what of the original central tower? Its risk of receiving serious damage would be far greater. That no more than the upper story of one of these can have fallen is evident from the fact that the south-western tower presents for examination to this day its original base, and the nature of the upper part of this same tower shows that it was rebuilt anew daring the first half of the thirteenth century. It was necessary that the two towers at the west as well as the central tower should be finished up to a certain level, for, placed as they were upon the plan, they became essential parts of the structure, whose absence would diminish the strength of the whole; hence any desire to maintain the fabric satisfactorily would require that those of them which fell should receive the immediate attention of the builders. In the case of the south-west tower we have already seen what was done, and obviously it was one of the two towers that had fallen. But what of the other of these? What suggestions remain to show which it was? It is well known that a central tower had been erected as part of the original plan, and also that a new upper part was being added to this same tower about the middle of the thirteenth century. This new portion eventually rose above the roofs to the level of the top of the square parapet, about the base of the octagonal spire, the spire being a still later addition. Now the heightening of this tower — perhaps with already the idea of a future spire in view — would raise many questions. Experience would already have taught the builders that the early central towers of many other churches were incapable of carrying their own weight. This being so, much less would it do to suppose that it could bear the addition of new weight upon the old piers; for though to all appearance sound, the cores were of rough rubble work, not solidly bedded and not properly bonded with the ashlar casing. So the question arises, did they remove the whole or part of the old central tower and piers, or were they saved this trouble by the structure having shared the fate of many others like itself, which fell, and so made way for new work? Another tower had fallen besides the one to which attention has already been drawn; and as there appears to be nothing to show that this other was the north-west tower, we must see what evidence there is concerning the central tower. That it was added to we already know. But documentary as well as structural evidence comes to our aid. The first is supplied by the records of Bishop Neville's episcopate; the next by the researches of modern archaeology. Professor Willis has shown in his remarks upon the structure of the piers at the time of the collapse of the mediæval tower and spire in 1861, that these had not been rebuilt at a date later than the twelfth century. But Mr. Sharpe[6], writing to Professor Willis seven years before the occurrence, indicates his discovery — from a close examination of the structure then existing — that before the upper part of the central tower was rebuilt in the thirteenth century the earlier arches at the crossing which were to support it had been taken down, and probably a large part of the piers carrying them. And that,

[5] Walcott, p. 15.
[6] Author of "Architectural Parallels."

though the twelfth-century voussoirs were re-used others of a fine grained stone were inserted among them to strengthen the arches, or as a substitute for some of the rougher sandstones that could not be used again. By this means, then, the original form and detail of the twelfth-century arches was preserved, so that the drawings representing the measured studies of the building, which were Sir Gilbert Scott's principal authority upon which to base his restoration of this portion of the tower, were made from work which had already been once rebuilt. But why was this part of the church rebuilt, and by whom? Two alternative suggestions for the reason have been offered.

Evidently, if the upper part of the tower did not fall, it is apparently certain that it was reconstructed, in order to carry the additional weight of the larger tower. But in examining the documentary evidence offered us, we find some further help. The teaching of archaeology shows that the portion of this tower above the main supporting arches and up to the bottom of the parapet was executed between 1225 and 1325—that is, it was finished not very long after the new part of the south-west tower was completed.

The cathedral statutes show that between the years 1244-1247 Bishop Ralph Neville was much concerned about a "stone tower" which he wished to see completed. They tell us, too, that the same bishop had himself expended one hundred and thirty marks upon the fabric,[7] and that his executors, besides releasing a debt of £60 due to him and spent on the bell-tower, gave £140 to the fabric of the church. Ralph died in 1244, so it is concluded that the work in which he was so interested was none other than the central or bell-tower of the cathedral, and that the earlier tower, with its supporting arches, must have fallen, else it is not likely that the work would have been rebuilt from below the spring of these arches before the new superstructure could be added; for we are obliged to take the customs of mediæval builders into consideration in any attempt to sift the evidence concerning their work—and they were before all things practical. The claims of structure, the motives of common-sense, rather than abstract and aesthetic ideals of beauty, were the prime causes at work in the evolution of their great art. Here they found themselves faced by a practical need—the rebuilding of a fallen tower. Its reconstruction was necessary to the completeness and stability of the building; so they put it up, applying new and increasing knowledge and skill in the execution of the work. They did their best, and the result was something not only strong and structural, but beautiful. But, as time has shown, it would have been better had they been less respectful of the valueless legacy bequeathed to them in the piers, though in defence of their sagacity it must be admitted that what they deemed sufficient for the purpose then in view was able to carry their own tower for five hundred years in safety, and not only this, but, in addition, a spire, the erection of which they may not have thought of when the restoration was begun.

There is another interesting fact which may be mentioned before quitting this part of our inquiry. Professor Willis found that there still existed in 1861 one of the old wooden trusses of the roof over the west bay of the chancel. It was a specimen of mediæval carpentry six hundred and fifty years old, and it had not, as he

---

[7] Walcott, p. 15.

showed, been unframed since the fire of 1186-1187. The timbers composing it had been slightly charred by the flames, and some of the lead which covered the burning roof had run in its melted condition into the mortices of the framing.[8]

In the admirable plan and sections which Professor Willis prepared to illustrate his work upon the history of the fabric it is possible to see at once what work had been done during the different stages of development. The work finished by the end of the thirteenth century changed the earlier church of the eleventh and twelfth centuries in its essential arrangements into the church we see to-day.

We have now briefly to review the changes produced in the plan of the cathedral. There were those effected as an immediate consequence of the fire, and others which were more the result of the continued energy of the thirteenth-century builders. The most remarkable one was that which converted the French chevet, or group of apses, into the more familiar square, and characteristically English, eastern termination. The apsidal chapels on the east side of each arm of the transept had disappeared to make room for others of a different shape and size. The other chapels at the east remained the same in number; but towards the close of the thirteenth century the lady-chapel had been lengthened, and the aisles of the choir, being continued eastward, ended in small chapels to the north and south of the central one. The other changes were those caused by the addition of chapels off the south and north aisles of the nave. The addition of the south and north porches, and the sacristy next to the south arm of the transept, were the only other alterations, if we except the addition of buttresses, which had been made in the original arrangement up to the beginning of the fourteenth century.

---

[8] See Willis, p. x.: Introduction.

From Winkle's Cathedral Churches.

THE CATHEDRAL FROM THE SOUTH-EAST, ABOUT 1836.

Though the quest may not be followed here, it would be interesting to try and trace the cause of this desire to add chapels to mediæval buildings. It had during the thirteenth century already become a clear indication of that gradual movement affecting the arrangement of churches which originated in the introduction of new doctrinal ideas. The particular set of ideas which caused such additions as these had now become a part of the common property of popular thought, imagination, and reverent superstition. The earlier designers and builders had not been taught to consider these features essential to the complete equipment of a church planned in accordance with primitive usages; they were a simple example of the influence which doctrine exercised upon the history of art and the scope of archaeological inquiry.

The course of history that has been followed has led us through the maze of some events which served to produce the cathedral that stands among us now. The later centuries will not require as much attention, since they afford but little material, comparatively, with which we need delay; for the industry expended upon the fabric since this time has produced little change in the general appearance of the building. With the approach of the fourteenth century we meet a period when the peculiarities of the work of the thirteenth century had become merged in transitional forms, and from this application of ever-developing ideas to accepted working principles came the well-known character which English architecture displayed during that time. It was native by parentage and birth; it represented the life which prevailed in the ideas which were then the common currency. By it the ideals of thought and imagination were expressed, until, later, they were represented in other forms of art. At Chichester an early indication of the changed treatment of older methods that was being developed experimentally is shown by the portion which was added to the lady-chapel during the episcopate of Gilbert de Sancto Leophardo. The architects and master-builders devised for him the two new eastern bays complete, together with the larger windows that were inserted in the walls of that part of the chapel already built. Here again, as in the work set in motion by his successor, the designers and builders made no attempt to add these new portions in imitation of earlier ones. Then it was Bishop Langton who, between 1305 and 1337, spent £340 "on a certain wall and windows on the south side, which he constructed from the ground upwards."[9] This work is principally to be seen in the great south window of the transept, under which he provided for himself a "founder's" tomb. In the gable above a rose window was inserted, following the example of that earlier one in the east end of the presbytery. The chapter-house above the treasury, or sacristy, was also added when the new windows were inserted in the lower walls. About the same time the doorway to the nave within the western porch was constructed.

---

[9] Bishop Reade's Register.

From Winkle's Cathedral Churches.

THE SOUTH TRANSEPT, ABOUT 1836.

Walcott shows by his study of the early statutes of the cathedral that "in 1359 the first fruits of the prebendal stalls were granted to the fabric; and in 1391, one-twentieth of all their rents was allotted by the dean and chapter to the works, which embraced works round the high altar, for, in 1402, materials 'ad opus summi altaris,' were stored in S. Faith's Chapel. A 'novum opus,' a term applied to some special building, was also in progress."[10] These remarks are of interest, since about the end of the fourteenth century a beautiful wooden reredos was built across the east end of the sanctuary. It was placed just west of the feretory of S. Richard. In many old prints its character is represented, and Dallaway gives some dimensions of it in the long section he shows of the church as it was before the reredos was removed (see page 2). The feretory no doubt had a reredos at this point, but what the type of this earlier arrangement may have been it is impossible exactly to tell. But the work which took its place was evidently beautiful, as the many remains still in existence prove to those who may examine them. Walcott[11] gives some interesting details concerning this work. From the representations, descriptions, and remains of it, it may be gathered that the whole was much carved, niched, and canopied, and decorated in colour; and there is a note extant showing that Lambert Bernardi in the sixteenth century repaired "the painted cloth of the crucifix over the high altar."[12] This reredos had a gallery across the top of it, from which the candles on a beam over the altar could be lighted and a watch kept over the precious jewels in S. Richard's shrine. The whole screen was made of oak, and those old sketches and drawings, or prints, of it still preserved, help dimly to show what had been its character. An old letter in the British Museum refers to it as having the finest "glory" above the high altar "we have ever seen." But this so-called "glory" was an eighteenth-century production. Much of the reredos is still hidden away unused in the chamber over the present library of the church, and since its first removal it has travelled as far as London in search of a friendly purchaser. In the chapter on Chichester in Winkles's "Cathedrals" a view in the "presbytery," dated 1836,[13] shows the reredos still in its place where it remained till after the fall of the spire. There are in existence two drawings of considerable interest.[14] One of these shows the east end and the other the west end of the choir as it was about the beginning of the last century (c. 1818); the other indicates what were the changes made after 1829, when the altar was set back six feet farther eastward. The latter was taken from a water-colour drawing supposed to have been made by Carter, an architect of Winchester.

Other minor works were added during the fourteenth century, but to few of these can any exact dates be assigned. The parapets to the north and south wall of the nave, the choir, and lady-chapel, and the painted oak choir-stalls were some of those additions.

In the fourteenth century we meet many changes in the treatment of the win-

[10] Walcott, p. 16.
[11] "Early Statutes."
[12] Walcott, p. 23, note a.
[13] See page 37-38.
[14] See drawings in vestry of cathedral.

dows. They became larger; they were themselves very treasuries of design, and this not only for the stonework of their tracery, but also for the very beautiful glass with which they had been filled. Their outer arches are more varied in shape, more rich in moulded detail, and the entire character of the curves of the moulded forms had been developed and made more delicate than the stronger and deeper-cut types from which they were derived. Two causes had apparently urged the builders to exert their capacities and apply their increasing technical skill to compass the aims proposed to them.

The small windows, the use of which had so long prevailed, did not admit sufficient light. In the more southern countries there was not the same reason for the change; but where light was less strong, less clear, less penetrating, it might not be spared. So though with their glass they were beautiful in themselves, many of these windows gave place to larger ones. But if the admission of more light was one reason for the change, there was another powerful inducement offered by the larger field that might be provided for the use of decorative colour, and they accepted the opportunity with alacrity—not as a mere chance for display only, but because, rather, they would be enabled to teach by the use of it.

But what was that *novum opus*, that special building that was already in progress in 1402? What was the reason for granting in 1359 the first-fruits of the prebendal stalls to the fabric? And in 1391 why did the dean and chapter give one-twentieth of all their rents to the works? And these works were not alone about the high altar, for the new work proceeding in 1402 had no doubt some relation to that which was in progress in 1391, and it can have been no mere small undertaking. Can these words be applied to the central tower and the spire that rose above it, or to the detached bell-tower of Ventnor stone northward of the church? It seems they must refer to the former, for to no other work can they be applied, since the angle turrets to the transept, the parapet of the central tower, and the windows inserted during the fifteenth century were not in existence at either of these times. And, further, the action taken in 1359 in order to provide funds for work that was proceeding could have no reference to the detached bell-tower, for its character shows that it was certainly not even begun before quite the end of the fourteenth century, probably not before some time during the first quarter of the fifteenth. So, since there was nothing else proceeding about the structure that could claim such sacrifice, the suggestion occurs that the spire was already in course of construction not long after the middle of the fourteenth century. The late Gordon M. Hills, Esq., in reporting to the chapter in 1892 his opinion concerning the condition of the fabric, said that, "Under Bishop William Rede (1369-1385) was begun a series of works: the completion of the central spire, the conversion of the north end of the north transept into a perpendicular work, the construction of a new library, the construction of the present cloisters, and finally the erection of the great detached belfry, called 'Raymond's, or Redemond's, or Riman's Tower,' was in progress in 1411, 1428, and 1436. All this work was carried on partly by the influence at Chichester of churchmen of the school of William of Wykeham, whose followers were strong at Chichester at this era."[15]

---

[15] See the Wykeham motto on the lady-chapel vault decoration, page *73-74*.

Photochrom Co., Ltd., photo.

THE BELL TOWER AND SPIRE AS SEEN FROM WEST STREET.

He also said "that the spire itself was commenced before the death of Bishop Neville. The moulding in the angles cannot, I think, have originated later"; and "that the early work extended to about forty feet above the tower; all the pinnacles and canopies at the base of the spire and the upper part of the spire, were insertions and rebuilding of one hundred years later. At the base the work of the earlier period had had its face cut away to bond in the later work, and the masonry of the two periods did not agree in coursing."

The mere fact that the detached tower was built suggests many questions which are not easily solved. Why was it at all necessary? Perhaps the cathedral bells hung in the south-west tower, and those of the sub-deanery church in the other, or *vice-versa*. At all events, we know that in the fifteenth century the sub-deanery church was removed from the nave to the north arm of the transept. The great window of the north end of the transept is also early fifteenth century in date, and the detached tower likewise. Angle turrets were placed upon the four angles of the transept during the same century; and if Daniel King's drawing of 1656 is any guide, the tops of the central and western towers had battlemented parapets added during the same period. In any case, it appears that it took much longer to complete the repair of the central tower than that at the south-west. In fact, it is doubtful whether the former was finished until about the end of the thirteenth or the beginning of the fourteenth century, for its fall apparently wrecked much of the vaulting of the transept; and this, from the character of its moulded and carved vaulting ribs in the south arm of the transept, is of the same date as the rose window in the east gable of the presbytery, the rose windows in the east gables of the lady-chapel and the chapels at the east end of the north and south aisles of the choir. This argues that at the end of the thirteenth or the beginning of the fourteenth century, during Bishop Leophardo's episcopate, these works were completed.

About the middle of the fifteenth century a stone rood screen was built up between the western piers of the central tower. It thus separated the choir under the crossing from the nave; but through the middle of this screen there was an open archway with iron gates. On either side, as parts of the screen, to the north and south was a chapel, each with its altar. This new work had been known as the Arundel screen, and its erection is often attributed to the bishop of that name, and at the altar in the south side of it Bishop Arundel founded a chantry for himself. Except that the cloister was added and some details of the building altered during the fifteenth century, no other architectural work of any size appears to have been done for many years.

DECORATION FORMERLY ON THE CHOIR VAULT.

From an engraving by T. King, 1814, lent by the Rev. Prebendary Bennett.
(Scale 7 feet 10½ in. to 1 in.)

The next work of importance was begun by Sherburne. He invited Lambert Bernardi and his sons to decorate the whole of the vaulting of the cathedral. This they did by covering it with beautifully painted designs. But unfortunately, excepting the small remnant now on the vault in the lady-chapel (see page 92), their work was entirely destroyed early in the nineteenth century. Some idea of its original beauty may be formed by an examination of similar work by other hands that may yet be seen in S. Anastasia at Verona, in two churches at Liege, and at S. Albans Abbey. An engraving by T. King, of about 1814, shows some details of the design that was painted on the vault of the choir in the bay next but one to the central tower. The cathedral was at this time an open book, with its walls covered with painted stories. The reredos, the stalls of the canons, as well as the walls, were rich with colour. Now all has gone except a meagre, faded scrap under the arch from the present library into the transept, and one or two other slight remnants. Sherburne also had some large pictures painted by the Bernardis. They represented the kings of England and the bishops of Chichester, and used to hang upon the west and east walls of the south transept.

From Sherburne's death until the seventeenth century little but a tale of destruction is to be recorded; for this period witnessed the dissolution of the monasteries, the beginning of a wholesale system of spoliation urged by self-interest and hypocrisy, and the establishment of "Reformation" methods of procedure in Church and State. By each of these both the fabric and the diocese suffered, even though by some they gained. But especially did vandalism help to destroy, unnecessarily, many things which, legitimately used, might still have been allowed to remain as evidences of the artistic influence of the Church in England. For though some of them were dedicated to uses which the reformation necessarily condemned the wholesale destruction of much beautiful workmanship must be regretted by any who are interested in such treasures. In 1538 it was ordered that all shrines should be abolished. This seriously affected Chichester, as the fate of the feretory of S. Richard was involved by the mandate. Two commissioners were named, whose duty was to see that his shrine was removed. The instructions issued served a double purpose, since in this case, as in others, "reformation" helped to satisfy the claims of avarice. Henry told the commissioners that

> "We, wylyng such superstitious abuses and idolatries to be taken away, command you with all convenient diligence to repayre unto the said cathedral church of Chichester and there to take down that shrine and bones of that bishop called S. Richard within the same, with all the sylver, gold, juells, and ornamentes aforesaid, to be safely and surely conveighed and brought unto our Tower of London, there to be bestowed as we shall further determine at your arrival. And also that ye shall see bothe the place where the same shryne standyth to be raysed and defaced even to the very ground, and all such other images of the church as any notable superstition hath been used to be taken and conveyed away."[16]

[16] Walcott, p. 34.

Then in 1550

> "there were letters sent to every bishop to pluck down the altars, in lieu of them to set up a table in some convenient place of the chancel within every church or chapel to serve for the ministration of the Blessed Communion."

Bishop Daye replied that

> "he could not conform his conscience to do what he was by the said letter commanded."

In explanation of his attitude towards this order he wrote that

> "he stycked not att the form, situation, or matter [*as stone or wood*] whereof the altar was made, but I then toke, as I now take, those things to be indifferent.... But the commandment which was given to me to take downe all altars within my diocese, and in lieu of them 'to sett up a table' implying in itselffe [*as I take it*] a playne abolyshment of the altare [*both the name and the things*] from the use and ministration of the Holy Communion, I could not with my conscience then execute."

The churches were so ransacked and destroyed in this way that Bishop Harsnett[17] said he found the cathedral and the buildings about the close had been criminally neglected for years, so that they were in a decayed and almost ruinous condition. Such was the deliberate opinion which he expressed early in the seventeenth century.

During the first half of the sixteenth century a stone parapet, or screen wall (taken away in 1829), was built up in front of the triforium arcade. It rose to a height of about four feet six inches, and was continued throughout the whole length of the church. It has been supposed that it was intended to render this gallery available as a place from which some of the congregation might observe the great ceremonials. So we see that after the close of the fifteenth century little but decline is to be recorded. Since Sherburne's day no care had been taken of the fabric; and except that an organ was introduced above the Arundel screen, no new schemes were devised, no new building done. It should be remembered, however, that the Reformation did not at once destroy all the beauties of mediæval art that the cathedral contained. Certain things, such as shrines, altars, chantries, and chapels, were removed, dismantled, or totally wrecked. It was with the coming of the Parliamentary army to the city that wholesale pillage and destruction began.

The removal of the altar and other derangements of the building had been effected during the preceding century; but now the vestments, plate, and ornaments were stolen. The decorative and other paintings on the walls, and all parts that could easily be reached, were scratched, scraped, and hacked about until they were mere wretched, disfiguring excrescences; and in this mutilated condition they waited for the whitewash that came later, to cover up these vulgar excesses with a cheap but clean decency. Such criminal procedure culminated in the wilful

---

[17] "Records."

wreckage of all the beautiful glass. The store of three centuries of labour and consummate skill was destroyed till it lay all strewn in broken fragments, mere rubbish, about the floors. But the decorations on the vaults were saved, because they could not be reached without expensive scaffolding. They were thus preserved to be dealt with by the wisdom and taste of a later century.

Let me quote the remarks of one who lived when these things were done. He says they

> "plundered the Cathedral, seized upon the vestments and ornaments of the Church, together with the consecrated plate serving for the altar; they left not so much as a cushion for the pulpit, nor a chalice for the Blessed Sacraments; the common soldiers brake down the organs, and dashing the pipes with their pole-axes, scoffingly said, 'hark how the organs go!' They brake the rail, which was done with that fury that the Table itself escaped not their madness. They forced open all the locks, whether of doors or desks, wherein the singing men laid up their common prayer books, their singing books, their gowns and surplices; they rent the books in pieces, and scattered the torn leaves all over the church even to the covering of the pavement, the gowns and surplices they reserved to secular uses. In the south cross ile the history of the church's foundation, the picture of the Kings of England, and the picture of the bishops of Selsey and Chichester, begun by Robert Sherborn the 37th Bishop of that see, they defaced and mangled with their hands and swords as high as they could reach. On the Tuesday following, after the sermon, possessed and transported by a bacchanalian fury, they ran up and down the church with their swords drawn, defacing the monuments of the dead, hacking and hewing the seats and stalls, and scraping the painted walls. Sir William Waller and the rest of the commanders standby as spectators and approvers of these barbarous impieties."[18]

This is a history in little of what took place in nearly every cathedral and other church in the kingdom, and this after the Reformation and its best work had been a fact for a century.

The most important disaster to the fabric during the seventeenth century was that which so seriously affected the structure at the west end. It is difficult to decide exactly when and how north-west tower fell or was removed. Professor Willis[19] is content to say:

> "Mr. Butler informs me that there is evidence to show that the north tower was taken down by the advice of Sir Christopher Wren, on account of its ruinous condition."

But Præcentor Ede, in a paper written about 1684 A.D. and quoted by Præcen-

---

[18] "Mercurius Rusticus" (1642). Quoted by Walcott.
[19] "Archaeological History," Chichester, p. 6, note c.

tor Walcott,[20] gives

> "an account of Dr. Christopher Wren's opinion concerning the rebuilding of one of the great towers at the west end of the Cathedral Church of Chichester, one third part of which, from top to bottom, fell down above fifty years since, which he gave after he had for about two hours viewed it both without and within, and above and below, and had also observed the great want of repairs, especially in the inside of the other great west tower, and having well surveyed the whole of the west end of the said Church, which was in substance as followeth; that there could be no secure building to the remaining part of the tower now standing; that, if there could and it were so built, there would be little uniformity between that and the other, they never having been alike nor were they both built together or with the Church, and when they were standing the west end could never look very handsome. And therefore considering the vast charge of rebuilding the fallen tower and repairing the other, he thought the best way was to pull down both together, with the west arch of the nave of the church between them; and to lengthen the two northern isles to answer exactly to the two southern; and then to close all with a well designed and fair built west end and porch; which would make the west end of the church look much handsome than ever it did, and would be done with half the charge."[21]

Such was Dr. Wren's opinion of the west front. It is fortunate that his advice was not followed, for have we not the same west front still in existence? However, Wren spoke of "the remaining part of the tower now standing," and King's print, publishing 1656, shows the portion to which he referred. Fuller[22] remarked in 1662 that the church "now is torn, having lately a great part thereof fallen to the ground." He no doubt refers to the same ruin, for it is not to be conjectured that any other part fell then.

Sir Christopher Wren says the towers never were alike in design, nor were they "both built together."

The edition of Dugdale's "Monasticon," published in 1673, gives a view of the north façade of the church. Ede, writing in 1684, said that "above fifty years" before one-third part of the north-west tower had fallen from top to bottom; yet this illustration shows that same tower complete. This affords an opportunity of comparing portions of the two towers. The upper part of each is shown to finish on top with a battlement parapet. It is evidence in itself that during the fifteenth century certain alterations had been effected in them both at this part. But this print must have been made from an original which had been executed quite twenty years earlier—for King's drawing, issued in 1656, shows the north-west tower already partly destroyed; so it is necessary to conclude that the drawing for the "Monasti-

[20] "Early Statutes," p. 21.
[21] Walcott, "Early Statutes" p. 21
[22] "Worthies," II, 385

con" was done before 1656, but after 1610, when Speed's map, or bird's-eye view, of the city was brought out.

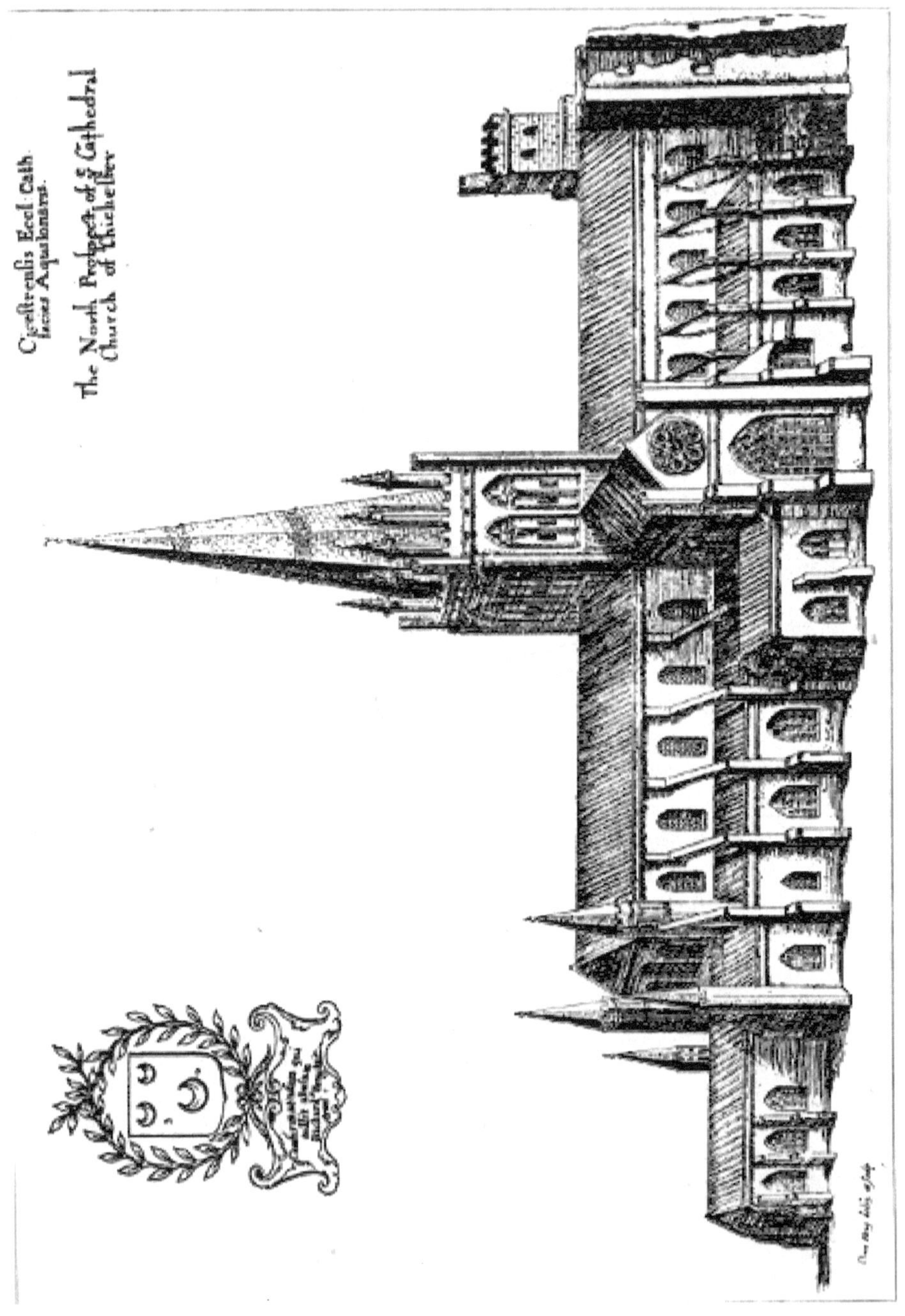

CHICHESTER CATHEDRAL, ABOUT 1650.

From an engraving by Daniel King.

Præcentor Walcott has supposed that the two towers in Chichester referred to in the "Annals of Dunstable" as having fallen during the year 1210 were the two at the west end.But taking Sir Christopher Wren's report with the discovery made by Mr. Sharpe in 1853, quoted by Professor Willis, it would seem rather that those two towers were the original central tower and that at the south-west angle of the west front.

Wren in writing of the tower at the north-west, which had fallen about 1630-1640, said that it had not been built at the same date nor in the same manner as the other then remaining to the south of the same front. The upper part of the central tower itself had been built perhaps during the second quarter of the fourteenth century or even earlier. Consequently it seems probable that the two towers which fell in 1210 were the original twelfth-century central tower and that of the same date to the south of the west front. In Speed's map of 1610 both the western towers are represented as having small spires.

Hollar's print in the "Monasticon" shows what appear to be some fifteenth-century buttresses to the north-west tower; but in excavating for the foundations of the new north-west tower, now completed, no traces of any projecting buttresses were discovered, so it may be that it was the original twelfth-century tower which fell about 1630, and the peculiar character of its masonry suggested the remark to Wren when he said it so distinctly differed from its companion.

Towards the close of the seventeenth century the central spire was in an unstable condition, and Elmes, in his "Life," says of Wren that he "took down and rebuilt the upper part of the spire of the cathedral, and fixed therein a pendulum stage to counteract the effects of the south and the south-westerly gales of wind, which act with some considerable power against it, and had forced it from its perpendicularity."

It is interesting to have this record, for the spire during the following century was still a cause of trouble.

Spershott's memoirs show that about 1725

> "a new chamber organ was added to the choir of the cathedral, the tubes of which were at first bright like silver, but are now like old tarnished brass."

Whether this organ contained any parts of that which was destroyed in the previous century is not known; but many old prints and drawings show that the case of the one that was now built on the top of the Arundel screen was quite as beautifully designed as the one in Exeter Cathedral, or King's College Chapel at Cambridge.

About 1749 the Duke of Richmond's vault was "diged and made"[23] in the lady-chapel, and ten years later "the kings and bishops in the cathedral" were "new painted." The floor of the lady-chapel was raised to give height to the vault beneath, and a fireplace and chimney built up in front of the east window. Portions of the other windows were plastered up, and so left only partly filled with glass.

---

[23] Spershott.

These served to provide light in what was now to be the library, since, apparently, the originally well-lighted library, above the chamber now used for the purpose, had lost its proper roof and been otherwise made useless.

There is little else to be said concerning the history of the building during eighteenth century; but it is stated by a careful observer,[24] writing in 1803, that "in the interior of this cathedral few innovations have been effected." He says that the east window of the lady-chapel is plastered up, and that

> "we find that the great window in the west front of the cathedral has a short time back had its mullions and other works knocked out, and your common masoned 'muntings' (mullions) and transoms stuck up in their room, without any tracery sweeps or turns, of the second and third degrees; which work may before long be construed by some shallow dabblers in architectural matters into the classical and chaste productions of our old workmen. On the north and south sides of the church are buttresses, with rare and uncommon octangular-columned terminations; but they have likewise, to save a trifling expense in reparation, been deprived of their principal embellishments, and are now capped with vulgar house-coping....
>
> "It may be well to speak of the west porch as an excellent performance; and the statue over the double entrance is remarkably so."

Proceeding, the same writer relates that:

> "Against the east and west walls of the said transept are affixed historic paintings; those on the west side (the figures as large as life) relate to the founding of the church and its re-edification in Henry viii.'s time. Among the various portraits is that of Henry viii. himself. Here are also in separate circular compartments, the quarter portraits of our kings, from William the Conqueror to Hen. viii. (and since his day, in continuation to George i.) On the east side is the entire collection of the ancient bishops of the see (quarter lengths, and in circular compartments). A short time back the faces of the several portraits were touched upon by some unskilful hand; however we have before us most curious specimens of the costume of Henry's day, when the whole of these paintings were done (excepting those of subsequent dates), in dresses, warlike habiliments, buildings, etc....
>
> "Looking towards the north, on the outside of the choir, is the monumental chapel and tomb of St. Richard. The groins above are embellished with paintings of foliage, arms, etc., conveying the eye over the choir; thence into the north transept, intercepted in the way by the galleries over the side-aisles, when the general combination of objects is terminated by the north transept win-

[24] Gentleman's Magazine, Part I., 1803, pp. 22-25.

dow, which, though inferior to the southern window, still has its own peculiar attractions."

At the time these words were written the north porch was in a wrecked condition. Both gables of the transept were in ruins, and the high-pitched roofs of the old library, the lady-chapel, and the south arm of the transept were absent altogether.

But soon the authorities began to take some interest in the condition of the building. James Elmes had been called in to deal with the spire in 1813-1814, and under his direction the "useful piece of machinery" which had been put there by Wren was "taken down and reinstated." In his "Life of Wren" an illustration is given of the device, which he had carefully examined and measured. He describes it thus:

> "To the finial is fastened a strong metal ring, and to that is suspended a large piece of yellow fir-timber eighty feet long and thirteen inches square; the masonry at the apex of the spire, being from nine to six inches thick, diminishing as it rises. The pendulum is loaded with iron, adding all its weight to the finial, and has two stout solid oak floors, the lower one smaller by about three, and the upper one by about two and a quarter inches, than the octagonal masonry which surrounds it. The effect in a storm is surprising and satisfactory. While the wind blows high against the vane and spire, the pendulum floor touches on the lee side, and its aperture is double on the windward: at the cessation, it oscillates slightly, and terminates in a perpendicular. The rest of the spire is quite clear of scaffolding. This contrivance is doubtless one of the most ingenious and appropriate of its great inventor's applications."

About 1814 T. King made a plan of the whole building and several drawings of the church as it then appeared. One of these[25] shows some carefully copied specimens of the decorations on the vaults. The engraving was published in 1831, and on it is the statement, "Painted 1520. Erased 1817." Another drawing showed the interior of the choir looking west. In this was represented in careful detail the design of the eastern elevation of the organ-case and the "return" stalls against the Arundel screen. It also shows the original iron gates in the archway, which pierced the screen in the centre below the organ, and formed the entrance to the choir. These gates were evidently copied in design from the thirteenth-century iron screen that protected the sanctuary, part of which is now in the Victoria and Albert Museum. In the distance the decoration on the nave vaulting is lightly indicated. There is also an original drawing by T. King in the possession of the Chapter, which gives a view looking eastwards. Another drawing[26] which was made some time after 1829 shows the choir looking east towards the reredos. It is a careful study, and is of peculiar interest, since it is a record of many features now entirely

[25] See illustrations, pp. 33 and 125.
[26] Supposed to be by Carter, an architect of Winchester.

removed. The early reredos appears still in its place, but the upper portion of it is gone. This was a gallery which was accessible from either triforium, across which boys early in the century used to run races by starting up the staircase in one aisle and down that in the other. The absence of the gallery in the drawing shows that it was made after 1829, the year in which the gallery was removed. The "glory" which was added to the reredos during the eighteenth century appears just above the altar. On the south side of the choir are some spectators in the gallery above the stalls. There were also at this time other galleries on the north and south of the sanctuary, and above the arch on the east side of the north arm of the transept was a gallery too. To this last there was access from the staircase that led to the chamber above the east chapel of the transept close by. These drawings show what the interior of the church was like up to the time when that extraordinary revival of activity in matters ecclesiastical began in the nineteenth century.

Like other churches, that at Chichester felt the sting of controversy in unnecessary vandalism. But it may be admitted that destruction, like a storm, carried at least some virtue in its clouds. In attempting to sweep away the accumulated refuse heaped within the building, some precious things fell before the broom of zealous furnishers, and were lost for ever in the dust raised by this new cleansing dream.

The removal of the gallery above the old fifteenth-century reredos in 1829 was the beginning of a serious attempt to repair, restore, and reanimate the fabric. This revival of faith began to try to do good works—but not always with discretion, not always with knowledge, wisdom, and taste. Here was rash ardour, often without the hesitation of true reverence.It is certain the building was not all it should have been when these works were begun; it is not what it might have been had some of them been deferred. Consequently any illustrations which show its condition before the middle of the nineteenth century are of interest and value to those who would know what changes have been made.

In Winkles's essay on Chichester, in his "Cathedrals of England," published between 1830 and 1840, are many beautiful drawings of the fabric. There is one which shows the Arundel screen still in its original position with the organ above it; and in another the complete design of the back of the reredos appears. These careful studies of the building, which were made before it became so changed by the removal of its best remaining treasures, help to convey some idea of what the place was before it was so radically "restored."

From Winkle's Cathedral Chruches.

THE NAVE, ABOUT 1836.

None of the drawings, however, show any of the beautiful decorations of the vaults, for all this had been smeared over with a dirty yellow wash about 1815, which earned for the church the name of "the leather breeches cathedral." And when, later, the plaster on the stone-filling between the ribs was removed, the paintings were utterly obliterated for ever, excepting only the small portion remaining in the lady-chapel bearing the Wykeham motto upon a scroll. But this recital is but a prelude to the changes that were to follow. The energy of revival found expression in many ways, and English architecture suffered sorely at the hands of ardent ignorance. But the very desire to deal well with the fabrics of our churches that were to be repaired taught men to study closely the facts of archaeology. The studies had a practical end, and at Chichester they found their opportunity in the cathedral.

From Winkle's Cathedral Chruches.

THE RETRO-CHOIR AND REREDOS, ABOUT 1836.

But first a new church of S. Peter was built in West Street in 1853, so that the north arm of the transept should no longer be used as it had been for about four hundred years. Then not long afterwards Dean Chandler, at his death, left a large sum to be used for the purpose of decorating the cathedral. To this sum other funds were added. The need that more space should be provided for the congregation arose, and to satisfy this it was decided that the choir should be opened out to the nave. Consequently, in 1859 the work of decoration was begun by the removal of the Arundel screen with the eighteenth-century organ above it—one of the most beautiful remnants of the art of earlier days that remained in the cathedral. The object of this act was most admirable, but it involved in addition the destruction of the fourteenth-century "return" stalls which were on the eastern face of the doomed screen. In taking down the screen, or shrine, all the stones composing it had been carefully numbered, with the intention that it should be rebuilt in a new position. But although these materials are still wantonly distributed about the cathedral and precincts, no attempt has been made to use them again, either as a screen or as an evidence to show by contrast that the result has justified the change. Its removal was the beginning of a series of alterations, both by accident and design. The old reredos, that quiet and beautiful witness of things so sacred and some so profane, was torn away. The whole of the choir was to be rearranged. But when the piers of the central tower were exposed by the removal of the screen, it was discovered that they were in a precariously rotten condition at the core. Other indications of weakness, which had been overlooked before, were now observed. Large and deep cracks and various earlier signs of apprehended weakness both in arches and piers were remarked. That the work now begun had given impetus to the fall has been denied on excellent authority, and to discuss such a question at this time is useless. The serious trouble now was that the whole tower with the spire was rapidly settling on its base. Every method that could be used was tried in order to save the piers. They were propped up with shores, and the arches held up with centres, while new masonry was bonded into the older work. But the labour availed nothing, for towards the end of the year 1860 matters had developed seriously.

> "Old fissures extended themselves into the fresh masonry, and new ones made their appearance.... But in the next place, the walling began to bulge towards the end of January 1861, first in the north-west pier, and afterwards in the south. Cracks and fissures, some opening and others closing, and the gradual deformation of the arches in the transept walls and elsewhere, indicated that fearful movements were taking place throughout the parts of the wall connected with the western piers."

On Sunday, February 17th,

> "the afternoon service was performed in the nave of the cathedral, as usual, but ... was interrupted by the urgent necessity for shoring up a part of the facing of the south-west pier.... On Wednesday, crushed mortar began to pour from the old fissures, flakes of the facing stone fell, and the braces began to bend. Yet

the workmen continued to add shoring until three hours and a half past midnight."

Next day the effort was resumed before daybreak; but by noon

"the continual failing of the shores showed, too plainly, that the fall was inevitable."

Just before half-past one

"the spire was seen to incline slightly to the south-west, and then to descend perpendicularly into the church, as one telescope tube slides into another, the mass of the tower crumbling beneath it. The fall was an affair of a few seconds, and was complete at half-past one."

Such, briefly, is the record of the fall, which so admirably has been related by Professor Willis, from whose work these extracts have been taken.

Sir Gilbert Scott,[27] after the central tower had collapsed, was consulted concerning its reconstruction. He examined the remains; and by the great care his son Gilbert exercised in labelling and registering all the moulded and carved stone that was discovered in the debris, the new tower and spire was designed upon the pattern of the old one. Old prints and photographs were used to help in this work of building a copy of what had been lost. But this task could not have been done had it not been that Mr. Joseph Butler, a former resident architect and Surveyor to the Chapter, had made measured drawings of the whole, which supplied actual dimensions that otherwise could not have been recovered. These drawings had come into the possession of Mr. Slater, the architect associated with Sir. G. Scott in the rebuilding of the tower, and they enabled him

"to put together upon paper all the fragments with certainty of correctness: so one thing with another, the whole design was absolutely and indisputably recovered. The only deviation from the design of the old steeple was this. The four arms of the cross had been (probably in the fourteenth century) raised some five or six feet in height, and thus had buried a part of what had originally been the clear height of the tower, and with it an ornamental arcading running round it. I lifted out the tower from this encroachment by adding five or six feet to its height; so that it now rises above the surrounding roofs as much as it originally did. I also omitted the partial walling up of the belfry windows, which may be seen in old views."[28]

These statements have been taken from Sir Gilbert Scott's own account of the work. He further assures us that many portions of the original moulded and carved work were re-fixed in the new tower. As we have now in existence so careful an imitation of the former tower, all praise is due to Sir Gilbert Scott, Mr. George Gilbert Scott, and Mr. Slater, for the admirable way in which they co-operated, so that

[27] See "Recollections," p. 309. Edited by his son, 1861.
[28] Ibid., p. 310.

their care has given to posterity this admirable instance in which a lost specimen of architectural art has been reproduced by successful copying. But the satisfactory nature of the work is chiefly due to the preservation of those careful studies of the original which were made by Mr. Joseph Butler.

In 1867 the wall enclosing the library in the lady-chapel was removed, and three years later, with the consent of the Duke of Richmond, the floor was lowered to its original level and the chapel restored in memory of Bishop Gilbert. Soon afterwards the windows were provided with new stained glass.

During the last half of the nineteenth century several small portions of the building were repaired, restored, or rebuilt. The cloister was carefully restored by the late Mr. Gordon M. Hills. More recently the roof of the lady-chapel, the two eastern pinnacles of the choir as well as those two lower ones to the chapels of S.M. Magdalen, and S. Catherine, have been restored by his son Mr. Gordon P.G. Hills, A.R.I.B.A., with much care and consideration for the fabric of which he is the surveyor. The latest act affecting the history of the building has been the addition of a new north-western tower to take the place of the unsightly rents and wreckage that have disfigured and helped to destroy the structure at that part during the last two hundred years. It was designed by the late Mr. J.L. Pearson, R.A.

Photochrom Co., Ltd., photo.

SOUTH-WEST VIEW OF THE CATHEDRAL FROM THE GARDEN
OF THE BISHOP'S PALACE.

CHAPTER II.

THE EXTERIOR.

As a design, the west front offers four important parts for observation; these are the two towers, the west wall of the nave proper, with the gable and the windows which compose it, and then the porch.

The **Towers** are now similar. The upper stage of that on the north is an imitation, as far as possible, of the same section of the other tower which was built in the thirteenth century. In its third stage some differences are introduced. The masonry of the new work is executed so as to carry on the courses of the old stonework that attach it to the rest of the front. The new work has followed the custom of the older and better traditions of the stonemasons, in that it has been left strictly as it was finished by the tool upon the "banker." The natural and simple texture imparted by the action of chiselling leaves a character upon the stonework similar to that of the earlier work.

The upper portion of the new north-west tower[29] being copied from that part of the old one to the south, it will be enough to describe the original. But first it is necessary to notice the lower stage of the southern tower. The buttressing on the south angle is of a later date than the rest of this section of the tower. It has a low weathered base. The central part of it has its projection at the base reduced when it reaches its summit by means of three steep sloping weatherings. There are also openings in the buttress for the staircase windows. The two lower windows of the west front in this tower are not placed in the same vertical line. This peculiarity has been followed in the new tower. The upper of these two windows is pointed, and has no label-mould. But the angle shafts that carry the arch have carved capitals and square-moulded abaci. Above the head of the pointed window the tower changes in character. The buttresses run up to the top as broad, flat surfaces, except that the northern one is slightly weathered twice. The coupled windows are more deeply recessed, having three orders of moulded arch-stones instead of the two, as in the lower window of a similar date; and the arch is carried by three shafts attached as parts of the jamb-stones. The windows have label-moulds over them, and the abaci of the capitals are carried across the buttresses on either side as a string-course. By this means the lines of the composition are continued horizontally, notwithstanding the interruption by the openings in the walling. These are now glazed as windows; but they were originally open, as some bells once hung in the tower at this level.

---

[29] By the late J.L. Pearson, R.A., and completed by his son.

S. B. Bolas & Co., photo.

THE NORTH-EAST ANGLE OF THE SOUTH-WEST TOWER.

The west end of the nave has six windows grouped in it above the porch. The two upper ones are small and close up under the gable coping. This latter is simply chamfered and capped with a modern cross. The windows are arched in two orders. The inner order has a plain, straight chamfered moulding; and the outer, a hollow chamfered one. The label-mould and the capitals of the attached shafts in the jambs are a little later in design than the windows themselves. A moulded string-course separates the point of the large west window from those above it; and from the level of this string-course up to the coping of the gable the whole surface of the wall is covered with a diagonal pattern of incised diapers.

The West Window is entirely modern, but copied from fourteenth-century examples with some success. It has five divisions between the jambs and mullions. The central one is larger than those on either side. The upper part is filled with geometrical tracery.

Below the west window are three other windows grouped together. They are at the triforium level, where they were probably inserted before the middle of the thirteenth century; but they have been restored at various times since then.

The **West Porch** is a comparatively simple structure. It rises from the ground with a deep weathered base. At the top of the walls is a plain weathered coping, which overhangs about one inch. The simple, but extremely well designed, buttresses at the north and south angles add much interest to it as a composition artistically and as a study in structure. The small, straight buttresses on the west are only weathered once, and this at the top; but those on the north and south sides are different. There is a broad central buttress weathered twice from the base to its top, and in the angle on either side of it are what appear to be two lower, smaller buttresses, with one weathering slope. The probability is that there was only a small buttress here at first, and that the larger one on either side was added by being built over the shallower, broader, and shorter one.These buttresses have been placed here in order to counteract the thrust of the large, deeply-set covering arch over the entrance to the porch. This arch is of interest, as it has but a slight label; and then the outside angle of the soffit only is moulded, the rest being recessed both at the jambs and in the arch for about two feet, with no mouldings at all. Then comes a delicately moulded arch in two orders, immediately beneath which are the coupled arches which give entrance to the interior, vaulted apartment. These two arches, the central and side shafts on which they rest, as well as the tympanum between them, are restorations.

The vault over the interior of the porch is carried on moulded diagonal ribs. On the north, south, and west are wall ribs as well, to carry the chalk filling between them. The insertion of two later monuments, now much dilapidated, involved the destruction of much of the beautiful wall arcades. These were of three complete divisions on each wall, and have cusped heads. The upper part, below the finishing horizontal string-course, is composed of two full and two half quatrefoils. The work in each arcade is recessed quite seven inches from the face of the general walling above; and the multiplied detail in the mouldings is finely studied. Opposite the entrance is the west doorway into the nave. The deep arch over this is seriously cracked in several places, though it has already been much restored. It has an outer label, which indicates that when it was built in there was then no porch to protect it. The three orders, or main groups, of mouldings do not run down on to the capitals, but finish by dying on to a plain piece of stonework of circular form set immediately upon the capitals. The Purbeck marble capitals themselves are rather large and heavily moulded, and the shafts under them are sandstone restorations of recent date. The west door and the woodwork about it is a poor specimen of modern ingenuity.

S. B. Bolas & Co., photo.

WALL ARCADE IN THE WEST PORCH.

The **South Side** of the church introduces many interesting varieties of work. These may well be followed in the course of this description from the west to the east end.

The lowest part of the south-west tower presents a treatment different from that on the west side. There is here a doorway, and an additional window. Both are round-arched. The doorway is one of the most notable pieces of beautiful design on all the exterior of the building. It is treated solely with variations of the well-known chevron ornament. The cut work upon it is in no case at all deep, but the total effect is truly delightful. There is none of the dead, formal regularity invariable in modern attempts to imitate this type of work. The voussoirs of the arch are not all of equal size in each order, and on one member the chevrons are reversed on opposite sides of the centre stone except for one accidental intermission. The abacus, nearly six inches deep, has a flat upper part on which a continuous diaper of Greek crosses has been cut. The lower part is a plain, hollowed chamfer moulding. Though the small columns in the jambs are new, and also parts of the inner reveal of the jamb, yet the old carved capitals are still in position and also the bases. These capitals bear distinct traces of Byzantine feeling in the design of them. Above the doorway is a billet-moulded string-course, which stops against the circular shafts by the buttresses, and forms the sill of the window. The design of this opening is like that of the one over it in the next stage, which is similar to that in the same position on the west face of the tower. But the abaci of its capitals run from the jambs across to the buttresses, as is the case with those of the doorway. The billet-moulded sill evidently passed round the tower completely, before the addition of the angle buttresses, since it appears again on the north buttress of the west front of the same tower; and the obvious inference is that there was once a window also on the west in this same stage at the same level. The window immediately below the upper division of the tower is of the same date and character exactly as the one on the west in the like place; and it should be noticed that the sills of the upper windows run on as string-courses, which are continued round the circular angle-shafts of the buttresses.

Passing eastward from the tower, the external **Roof** of the nave becomes visible. The irregularly waved line of the ridge where the lead rolls meet, as it were, against the sky, is a pretty indication of the presence of the aged timbers underneath that support it above the walls.

The oldest part of the building to be seen from this point is the strip of walling at the clerestory level. The twelfth-century round-arched windows are there almost complete. In detail they are like those of the tower. Two of them, those in the fourth and fifth bays from the tower, have had later work inserted in the same openings.

The crest of the wall between the west and the central tower was renewed in the fourteenth century. It consists of a parapet with a weathered coping for the top course of stonework, so that the water might not rest upon it and percolate through the walls. Three courses below this is a simply moulded string-course, and immediately beneath is the cusped arcade supported on the course of detached moulded and shaped corbels. For five feet below the bottom of the corbels the newer part of the wall is continued. It will be interesting later to notice the way in which the parapet on the north side of the nave has been dealt with. The reason for the presence of so much new walling at this level is no doubt to be found in the fact that the roof timbers at the time of the second fire were carried down over the walls.

The water from the gutter behind the parapet is carried out on to the backs of the flying-buttresses by means of holes cut through the stonework. Into these pipes are passed which convey the water through to the open gutter channels of the buttresses. The backs of the raking buttresses, though they are sharply weathered to throw the water from them quickly, are also covered with lead as a further protection. These buttresses have carried the thrust of the vaults down-wards with safety for about six hundred years. But the presence of two distinct arches under each of them indicates that they have been altered a little since first they were put up. This was done when it became necessary to carry their thrust farther out because of the new chapels that were added long after the vaults were built over the nave. At the foot of each raking slope is a horizontal piece which runs out until it comes in contact with the octagon pinnacles of the vertical exterior buttresses. It should be noted that where the flying-buttresses meet the vertical wall of the clerestory there is in some cases a portion of the flat buttressing of the twelfth century visible.

Between the buttresses of the chapels are four two-light windows, The outer arch of each of these windows is a beautiful example of late thirteenth-century moulded detail. The main line of the arch curve is excellent, and the whole opening between the head, jambs, and sill is beautifully proportioned. Some fifteenth century tracery remained in these windows until it was replaced by the present modern work. The outer arch is in two orders, which are carried by slight attached shafts, some of which are renewals. The capitals to these are carved, and have square abaci, rounded at the angle, as they pass over the capitals. These abaci, which are finely moulded, are not more than about two and a half inches in depth. The bases of the jamb-shafts are characteristic of the period during which this work was done. There are two small rounded mouldings, and one larger one. These rest on the square, lower part, of the base. Immediately below the sill is a string-course; and this, as well as the projecting base to the whole wall, is continued from the side of the tower buttress eastward. Each is returned round the four buttresses till it stops against the outer wall of the south walk of the cloisters. The vertical buttresses here were originally completed with a weathering at a point about half-way up their present height; and upon this old weathering the upper and later part of the buttress has been added. This was probably done during the fourteenth century, about the time that the adjoining parapet of the aisles, the parapet of the nave, and the re-working of the upper part of the flying-buttresses was undertaken. This change in the design involved the removal of the range of pointed gables, by which the roof over each bay of the aisle was completed southward. Traces of the earlier gable copings are still bedded in their original places in the walling. Upon three of these buttresses are remains of the old gargoyles by which the water from the roofs was carried off. The use of these is now superseded by the cheap and mean-looking rain-water heads and pipes.

Close by the parapet of the aisle the square angles of each buttress are cut off so as to form a base for the octagonal pinnacle above. These, when in their complete state, were undoubtedly very beautiful; for besides what can be now seen, it is known that they were once completed each with a spirelet. Now they have the substitutes suggested by parsimony to cover their incompleteness. As they are, in their ruined condition, it may be seen that they were not all finished in identically the same way. The three sides on the north of the octagon of each one are left plain and flat. The other five sides are treated as narrow, recessed panels, formed by the six groups of small shafts at either angle. Every group has its capital and moulded base. The capitals in some cases are carved, in others moulded only. Above each capital is a small carved boss. This, doubtless, was the stop to some member on the angles of the spirelets. Springing from the capitals are moulded and cusped arches, which form on either side the heads of the panelled divisions. The horizontal part of the weathering of the flying-buttresses is stopped behind the octagons of the pinnacles.

The parapet has a plain weathered coping, close under which is a string-course which helps to throw the water clear from the top of the wall; and two coupes below this one is another moulded string. Each is about six inches in depth. If is not possible to state more concerning these parts in detail, since they have been much repaired at various times.

The stove-pipes which run up the north and south sides of the nave as smoke-flues for the heating-apparatus do not add to the beauty of the exterior.

In the fifth bay, eastward from the south-west tower, is the **South Porch**, which opens directly into the west walk of the cloister. Early in the nineteenth century it was in a ruinous condition; but restoration has again given it stability, if not all its old beauty. The idea of the design, as it is seen from the cloister, is identical with that of the exterior of the west porch. But in the detail of its mouldings and other features it is different entirely. The restored abaci of the capitals, like the originals, are some of them square, others irregular octagons. The interior is vaulted, and has diagonal and wall ribs. On the west and east sides are stone benches. But the west side has in addition a small arcade of four arches forming recessed sedilia. The mouldings to the arches of this small arcade are of about the same date as those in the two outer orders of the enclosing arch on the south front of this porch. The two smaller arches under it appear to be later work, if we judge from their present character. But the arch-mould of the **Doorway** within the porch is work of approximately the same date as the outer moulded member of the enclosing arch on the west front of the west porch. The enclosing arch of the south porch is later work than these. But the two inner moulded orders of the enclosing arch of the west porch are even later still in character.

The east side of this south porch forms the west wall of the present choir singing school—the old sacristy. But this room projects farther southward than the porch. The limit of its projection is indicated by a portion of a buttress in the cloister. Between this buttress and the porch are two small windows—one of them is now blocked up. The upper one is the same in design as those others on the south side of the same apartment. These we shall consider presently. Above the central pier at the entrance to this porch is a miserable figure in stone, intended to represent a saint.

S. B. Bolas & Co., photo.

THE SOUTH DOORWAY IN THE WEST WALK OF THE CLOISTER.

The **Cloister**, which was added in the fifteenth century, is of a peculiarly irregular shape, and encloses the south transept within the paradise. It has been much restored at different times. The present roof is of tiles, and is carried on common rafters. Each has a cross-tie, and the struts are shaped so as to give a pointed, arched form to each one. The old fifteenth-century wooden cornice still remains in some sections. The walling was once all plastered. The tracery is divided into four compartments by mullions, and each head is filled with cusped work.

Round the cloister are placed the old houses of the Treasurer, the Royal Chaplains, and Wiccamical Prebendaries. Above the door leading to the house of the Royal Chaplains is an interesting monument of the Tudor period. It is a panel divided into two compartments by a moulded stone framework.

S. B. Bolas & Co., photo.

THE WEST WALK OF THE CLOISTER FROM THE SOUTH-EAST.

Leading out of the south walk is a doorway, through which the deanery may be seen beyond the end of a long walled passage known as S. Richard's Walk. Looking back northwards, there is a fine view of the spire and transept from the end of this walk.

The chamber over the present singing school between the south arm of the transept and the west walk of the cloister shows the effect produced by some changes made during the fifteenth century. The masonry was more carefully finished than that of the adjoining transept—a specimen of twelfth-century work. The joints in the later work are thinner, and the average size of the stones is in this case smaller.

On the south side of the wall of this chamber are two buttresses. Close under the shallow moulded coping at the top of the wall are two fifteenth-century windows. They are not placed centrally over the others below. In design they are each divided into three lights by mullions. On the east side of the middle buttress is an old rain-water head of (eighteenth-century?) leadwork. Part of the lead piping still remains, having the old ears to fasten it to the walls. The west side of this chamber has one buttress on the south angle and a window in the centre of the wall. Above it is the low slope of a gable. The window is similar to those on the south side, but the head is a pointed and four-centred arch. The mullions have been restored. Below the part just described is the earlier work of the thirteenth century. It rises as far up as to the string-course formed by the continuation of the abaci of the capitals in the two small single-light windows. These narrow and sharp-pointed windows are peculiar. The arch-moulds are different from the other work of the same date in the church. There is no sign of tracery in their design, and the jambs have a simple attached shaft in the outer reveal. The bases to these shafts are earlier than those of the shafts to the south aisle chapel windows, and the edge of the inner member of the window arch is merely cut off with a straight chamber. There is one window, the same as these, hidden in the west walk of the cloister. Beneath the windows just described there are two small single-light openings in each portion of walling on either side of the central buttress. These six windows serve to light the vaulted (sacristy) choir school within.

It has been supposed by some that a chapter-house once existed within the paradise close by the west angle of the transept. The south end of the transept rises on the north side of the cloister garth. At the south-west angle a great part of the twelfth-century masonry in the broad flat buttresses remains. The south-east angle and buttresses are quite different. They are perhaps part of the work done during the thirteenth century, though it is possible that they were introduced when Langton inserted the large south window of the transept. This window has been very much restored since the seventeenth century, when it was almost knocked in pieces. Wooden props served instead of mullions for many years to hold up the tracery above. The repair that has been effected retains the old design. Above each angle of the transept is a turret, octagonal in form. Neither of them is complete. They were only required in the fifteenth century as a means of access to the roofs at the parapet level from the staircases in the angle buttresses. The gable of the transept rises above the parapet just described, but it is not in the same vertical plane as the face of the wall below. The top of this gable was for many years in a very wrecked condition. The design of the tracery in the rose window is in two orders, based upon equilateral triangles filled in with cusps.

S. B. Bolas & Co., photo.

THE EAST WALK OF THE CLOISTER.

Close to the ground on the south-west corner buttress are two string-courses. The lower of these is a billet-moulded course cut, like those to be seen on the south-west tower. Its presence here, and at this level, shows that this was the original level of the sills of all the old Norman windows on the outside walls until about the close of the twelfth century.

On the east side of this part of the transept, at the clerestory level, are two round-headed windows. Both originally were all of twelfth-century workmanship. But now the southern one has abaci, capitals, angle-shafts, and base, which are thirteenth-century work, and the early label-mould has been changed. The other window shows partly what was once probably the character of both of them. But the greater part of this window was restored when the central tower and spire were rebuilt after 1861. Between the windows is a buttress that was introduced when the vault was added. The south-east angle on this side retains part of the twelfth-century flat buttressing. There are on this wall and the turret different types of masonry, which represent five distinct periods of building, from the twelfth to the nineteenth century. But the junction between the work of two of these periods, being a weak part, shows by the crack down the wall from the parapet that some movement has taken place here.

Projecting eastwards from the transept is the square chapel (now a vestry), which took the place of the early apsidal one. Neither of its three windows has any tracery. The window on the south side is pointed. The arch-mould is the same as that to the round-headed window on the east; but there is a label-mould over this south one and not on the other. The abaci are new, and the angle-shafts and bases as well, but the capitals are old, though decayed. The parapet on the south is of the same character and date as that over the wall of the choir, but earlier than that above the south window of the transept, which is of the same date as that on the south wall of the nave.

The roof of this chapel appears, from the raking channel on the transept wall, to have once been higher, with a sharper pitch. The finish to the present gable point has disappeared. On the east wall and on the south-west buttress of the transept there are two interesting old lead rain-water heads. The east wall of the chapel runs on northwards till it becomes a part of the buttress of the choir. The wall between the north buttress of the chapel and the buttress of the choir aisle close by is pierced with two small cusped windows of fifteenth-century date. Below these is a larger and sharply pointed arched head. It has no mouldings. But the square-headed small light under it has splayed jambs. This opening was probably once a round-headed twelfth-century window, as the old abacus is still in position.

The **South Side of the Choir** is externally divided into five bays. There are five flying-buttresses to carry down the vault thrusts, with a pinnacle above the buttress at the south-east angle. The first, second, and third bays from the east side of the transept have still the round-arched windows of the twelfth century set in the walling of the same date. But it should be noted that part of the window in the first bay was rebuilt after 1861. The fourth and fifth bays have pointed windows, carved capitals, and angle-shafts. These, though now entirely renewed, were built when the whole of this part of the choir was added. Part of the walling for a few feet below the parapet was renewed at the same time. The flying-buttresses are thirteenth-century additions of the same date as the vaults within; and those three nearest the transept abut on parts of the twelfth-century flat buttresses. The flat projection was continued up to the parapet at a later date, probably when the parapet itself was built on. But the fourth buttress also abuts upon a slightly projecting flat strip of buttressing. In this case, however, but not in the others, the flat strip and the flying-buttress are of the same width and built as one piece of structure. The third and fourth flying-buttresses have a secondary, and apparently later, arch of fine grained white stone beneath their larger arches.

The copings on the backs of these buttresses are not weathered like those of the nave, and, except the one next the transept, each is covered with lead. There are no pinnacles to them above the aisle wall. The fourteenth-century builders had not touched them, as they did those south of the nave. There are, too, no gutters along their backs. It is curious that this method of carrying the water away from the upper roofs over the lower ones should not have been adopted when the parapets were put up.

S. B. Bolas & Co., photo.

THE CHOIR AND CENTRAL TOWER FROM THE SOUTH-EAST.

The outer wall of the choir aisle is one of the most interesting portions of the building, from an archaeological as well as an architectural standpoint. It shows three of the arched heads of small twelfth-century windows that used to light the earlier triforium gallery. One of these has now a fifteenth-century insertion beneath it. This is in the second bay from the transept. It is a small window with a cusped head and a square label-mould above it. In the same area of walling there are shown the levels of the cut string-course that ran along under the sills of the twelfth-century aisle windows. It is the same string and at the same level as it appears upon the south-west angle of the transept and the south-west tower of the west front. It shows, too, in the second bay, the level of the old abaci which ran across from each capital in the window jambs and stopped against the sides of the buttresses. There is also the continuous chamfer course that ran along the walls above the heads of these aisle windows. In proof of these things there is even now one of these same old windows in almost its original state within the little chamber known as the priest-vicars' vestry. This window is in the bay of aisle walling immediately against the transept wall. The string-courses of the old windows were continued round the later buttresses. In the fourth bay, above the point of the window arch, the curve of the original apse of the ambulatory is just traceable; but beyond this point eastwards the twelfth-century walling has disappeared until we meet it again in the lady-chapel. There is a small buttress in the fourth bay marking the junction between the two periods of masonry. In the second and third bays part of the twelfth-century top to the aisle walls remains. The roof may have had eaves originally, but now there is a parapet of about the same date as the present buttresses; and the projection of this parapet is carried upon the corbels that were carved and built in before the second fire occurred. The space between each corbel is bridged over by small single stones cut out to the shape of a semicircular arch.

The windows in the second, third, and fourth bays differ in size and shape from each other; that in the second bay has a pointed arch and no tracery, square abaci and the remains of carved capitals. The angle shafts and bases are gone. They were all inserted at about the same time; but that in the third bay has had some poor modern tracery without cusps added to it, and that in the fourth bay is a more recent, insertion than the one next to it. In the third and fourth bays just above the low chamfered base of the wall are three semicircular markings cut on the wall, but there is nothing to explain their existence. In the fourth bay close beneath the sill of the window is a stone built into the wall, upon which a dedication cross is cut. At the fifth bay the east walk of the cloisters joins the wall of the aisle; its roof partly hides a window, above which is a square panel of the fifteenth century. This panel indicates the position of a window, for the jambs and mullions of its tracery may be seen within the church. They are rebated for shutters, the old hooks for which also remain. The south-east angle turret of the presbytery has lately been rebuilt; so also has that on the north-east angle. They are each of them octagonal in form, but differ in detail, in imitation of those they replace.

The large rose window in the gable of the **East End** is of about the same date as the vaulting over the south transept, since they possess kindred details. In design it is a simple circle, with seven others within it of equal diameter. Portions of the coping of an earlier and lower pointed gable are bedded in the wall. Under the string beneath the rose window are three windows grouped as a triplet, with no label moulding. The centre light is higher than the others. Though each has been much repaired, the early thirteenth-century detail has been retained. The abaci of the capitals are square. The windows have no tracery, and are probably quite fifty years earlier in date than the large rose above them.

The exterior of the small chapel to the south has a square weathered angle buttress. On its south side is a window of the same date as the rest of the chapel, and like the triplet in the gable of the presbytery in character and date. Its east end has been altered since the chapel was finished. First a small rose window, recently renewed, of the same date and type as that in the presbytery gable, was inserted under the earlier narrow window close to the gable point; then the original east window was removed, and a larger one was put in, having three lights and a traceried head with cusped work of late fourteenth-or early fifteenth-century work. The sill of the old window was lowered to give more length. Most of the window now to be seen is the result of recent restoration. Parts of the old string-courses remain in the walling.

The south side of the **Lady-Chapel** beyond the chapel just described has four bays. In each of these is a large three-light window. The western and smallest one was probably first inserted. Then the two eastern ones were put in when the two east bays were added to the older lady-chapel. The other window appears the latest of the four; or else may it not be that before deciding to lengthen the lady-chapel, the builders first began only with the idea of inserting some new windows in the older walls? But before this scheme had been executed they concluded that they would add bodily to the chapel; and in order to allow the chapel to continue in use while this was being done, they built the extension first outside, then built up the connection with the original walls, and inserted their latest window. Two of the buttresses on this wall are flat. In this they are like those of the twelfth century; but their upper parts were rebuilt when the parapet was made. The others are later, and have more projection. On the north and south of the lady-chapel the wall is finished by a parapet. It is the same in detail and design as that on the south wall of the presbytery. So it is probable that Bishop Gilbert de S. Leophardo, when he lengthened the lady-chapel, caused other work to be done at the same time.

The lady-chapel has been much restored in many ways, but the old parapet remains in part on the north side. The tracery of the windows is interesting, as it shows early examples of cusped forms. The east end of the lady-chapel has a five-light window, which has been much repaired. It has been in a measure imitated from the others in the chapel.

The description of the south side of the chapel applies generally to the north side. But the windows in two cases have been much more restored. The chapel north of the lady-chapel has an angle turret like that on the south. Its east and north windows are fifteenth-century insertions. And it has a little rose window in the gable not yet restored, though soon, by decay, it will have disappeared. The smaller window above it is blocked up. On its north side there is neither a gutter nor a parapet; but perhaps this is better than the foolish cornice, with rosettes in it, which has been placed on the wall of the south chapel to carry a gutter.

S. B. Bolas & Co., photo.

WINDOWS OF THE LADY-CHAPEL, SOUTH SIDE.

The details of the north wall of the presbytery are similar to those described on the south. But there are no sub-arches to any of the flying buttresses, and the slopes of each are protected by lead coverings. And in the exterior of the north aisle the same elements of structure and design may be discovered, even to the presence of twelfth-century remains, the curve of the old encircling apse, and the position of the first sills, abaci, and string-courses. But it should be noticed that in the eastern bay of this aisle externally, where on the south there is a fifteenth-century solid square panel, on the north there is a small round-headed window. But this little window is of no earlier date than the walls in which it is set. The second and third windows from the east buttress of the presbytery aisle are insertions of fifteenth-century type; but they have been so much renewed and restored that only in the third one does there appear to be any portion of the original tracery remaining. On the north side of the choir and presbytery are four very fine old lead rain-water heads and square lead pipes.

The east end of the present **Library** has in it five windows. Two of the upper ones are built up, the central and higher one only being glazed. In detail they are all of the same date as the walls they are in. None has any tracery, and by this they show that this piece of work was done at the same time as the chapel—now a vestry—on the east side of the south end of the transept. The gable is a low slope like the present roof, but the slope of the old gable and roof may be seen upon the east wall of the transept. There is one buttress only on the east side of the library. The north side is divided into two parts in its length by a buttress. The parapet has a corbel course similar to that on the two eastern bays of the presbytery aisle. The two small pointed windows below it are built up, as now the apartment they once lighted is a lumber-room, where the remnants of the old reredos are stored. The larger windows below are of the same date, nearly, as those two fifteenth-century ones in the north wall of the presbytery aisle. The east one has three and the west four lights, with cusped tracery in the heads.

The east wall of the north arm of the **Transept** has a buttress, as is the case with the south arm. But early thirteenth-century pointed windows take the place of the round-headed ones. There are, however, three string-courses on this wall of the north arm which do not appear on the south. One is the old twelfth-century string which evidently once ran along above the old round-headed windows. The next is a continuation of the abaci of the capitals. The other passes under the sills of the windows. A comparison of this wall with that corresponding to it in the south of the transept shows that for some reason the windows here were totally changed and the others only partially. This may suggest that at the time of the fire this part was more damaged than the other. The parapet on this wall is unlike that at the top of the presbytery and choir walls. It has no corbelling and no arched and cusped work; it is merely a plain piece of walling, slightly overhung with a weathered coping at the top and a moulded string beneath.

The general features in the design of the north end of this transept are similar to those of the south. The gable sets back from the face of the lower wall as before, and in it is a rose window, also based on the hexagon principle in design. It is later in character than either of the other large rose windows in the south of the transept and the east of the presbytery. Like the others, it has been much repaired. The two irregular octagon turrets on each angle are of the same date as those on the south, and, like them, have weathered and battlemented parapets to the top of their side walls. The parapet of the north wall between them is of the same design, detail, and date as that on the north and south walls of the clerestory to the nave.

On the north-east angle are two buttresses; and on the north-west angle there is a group of buttresses of a later type. On the west there remains the old twelfth-century flat buttress, like those on the south-west angle of the transept. Westward of this, and standing clear of the wall, is a fine fourteenth-century flying-buttress. Projecting northwards, but attached to the north-west angle, is a vertical buttress of the same date as the flying one close to it.

On the west side, this part of the transept almost repeats what is to be observed on the east; but the parapet here is the same as that on the north end, and near the ground is one of the twelfth-century windows. The arch-mould of its rounded head is the same in detail as those in the priest-vicars' vestry and in the chamber above the present library. It seems to be an example of that later work of the twelfth century of which other specimens no doubt remained in the walls of the lady-chapel before Bishop Gilbert transformed it into its present state. Close to this window, and rising up just above the sill of the clerestory windows, is a narrow, flat buttress, which is probably of the same date as the window. Its upper half has an attached shaft on each angle, with moulded bases and carved capitals of the same period; but the weathering on its top appears to have been changed in the thirteenth century.

Close by is the only part now remaining of the twelfth-century outer wall of the nave aisle. The original corbel course of the parapet remains, but not the upper part of the parapet. And it may be seen here that the small windows that lighted the triforium gallery had round arched heads in two orders, with a string-course at their sill. Below this string is a thirteenth-century pointed window, with a billet-moulded label cut in a twelfth-century manner of design.

The north side of the nave retains the seven twelfth-century clerestory windows, the one next to the transept having been rebuilt after the fall of the central tower and spire in 1861. There are no remains of later insertions, as on the south side. The parapet is later in design than those to the choir and lady-chapel; but it is of the same date as that on the south wall of the nave. In the five eastern bays it is of two tiers. The upper projects beyond the lower, and so widens the span between the north and south clerestory walls. It has been suggested that this was done in order to straighten the north wall, which in the twelfth century had been built so that it bent inwards towards the south.

The weathered and channelled backs of five of the buttresses are the same date as those south of the nave; but the easternmost one has a flat raking back like those to the north and south of the choir and presbytery. The four western buttresses had pinnacles with spirelets—now destroyed. The western one was square, the other three octagonal. All these are earlier in date than the fifth one from the west, this last one being probably the same in date, as it is in detail, as those on the south side. The sixth one finishes plainly with a square top. It may once have had a pinnacle, but none now remains.

The parapet to the aisle chapels in the four western bays is plain, with a weathered coping and string-course in which is some carved work of late fourteenth-century date. The gables between the buttresses are gone, as is the case on the south side; but traces of their old copings remain. The four large three-light windows are the same in design and detail, and were no doubt executed when the chapels themselves were built. They have traceried heads with early types of cusping of about the same date as, or a little later than, the rose window in the east gable; but they are certainly thirty or forty years earlier than those of the lady-chapel. The north window of the chapel in the fifth bay is a modern insertion of the same character as in the south aisle chapels of the nave. It probably, like them, contained a fifteenth-century window, which was removed to satisfy the taste which thought the present substitute the better thing. The detail of the two orders of its outer arch is earlier than that of the windows west of it. Above the point of this window is a small circular one, with a cusped treatment of perhaps the same date as the ones in the east end of the chapels at the end of the aisles of the presbytery.

Photochrom Co., Ltd., photo.

THE CATHEDRAL FROM THE NORTH-EAST.

The **North Porch** has a pointed outer arch in two orders. The abaci to the capitals are square; but now there are no shafts or bases in the jambs. The sub-arches appear to be about the same date as the transept vaulting, as they have the dogtooth ornament in their mouldings. On the west face of the buttress, close by, is a double niche in very bad repair; but as a specimen of work it is well worth studying. The parvise chamber above this porch is not lighted except by the small cuttings in the form of a cross which pierce the wall.

The new north-west tower, or its north front, has imitations of twelfth-century work throughout, except in the case of the coupled openings in the top stage, which are like the thirteenth-century work at the same level in the south-west tower. The lower part of the north-east buttress incorporates the remains of the original twelfth-century flat buttressing.

The **Central Tower** and **Spire**, although they were rebuilt again after the disaster in 1861, are as nearly as possible an exact reproduction of the originals.

The tower rises out of the substructure where the roofs of the nave and transept intersect. It is not square in plan, but has an axis from east to west, longer than that from north to south. Below the string-course, under the weathered sills of the arcaded openings in the belfry stage, are, on the north, south, and west, small wall arcades. At each angle there is a turret. Three of these are octagonal, but that at the south-west is circular till it reaches the string course below the parapet; and excepting those on the north-west and south-west they are used as staircases. Each of the four sides is pierced by two groups of coupled openings under superior arches, the several moulded members of which rise in four receding orders from the square abaci of the capitals of the angle shafts. The space between the pointed heads of the sub-arches on the east and west faces is pierced by quatrefoils; those on the west are different in design from those on the east.

The parapet of the tower has features in its design which indicate that the original one W been added to the earlier tower during the fifteenth century. The octagonal terminations to the four turrets were of the same character and date as the parapet.

The spire rises out of the supporting walls of the tower within the parapet. It is a regular octagon in shape. Four octagonal pinnacles are placed at its base next to each of the turrets of the tower; and between these, on the other four faces of the spire, are tall stone dormers, with carved crockets and finials on the copings of the high-pitched gables. Above this group the spire is divided into three sections by two bands of diaper-work cut out of the stone surfaces as cusped quatrefoils; and from the base of the spire to its capstone there is a projecting rib on each angle between the several faces of the octagon.

THE DETACHED BELL-TOWER.

The **Bell Tower**, which stands alone to the north of the cathedral, is now the only one of its kind in England; and it is curious that in two cases where these towers were found, as at Salisbury and at Norwich, spires had been added to the central towers. The cathedral bells have been hung in this tower since the fifteenth century. The structure itself, with its massive walls, is square in plan at the base, but at the top story it becomes an octagon, and the buttresses on each angle terminate as pinnacles between the angles of the square and four sides of the octagon.

Photochrom Co., Ltd., photo.

THE NAVE, LOOKING WEST.

CHAPTER III.

THE INTERIOR.

The **Nave** of Chichester, compared with that of other cathedrals, possesses several peculiar characteristics. It has a beauty apart from others in the quiet simplicity with which it has been designed. There is an evident restraint, almost severity, to be felt in studying the exquisite proportions of its parts. It does not exhibit the massive force and strength of Durham; but the rigid power in the square piers of the arcades is stern compared with the more subtle variations of light and shade produced by the curved surfaces of the circular piers either at Ely or Peterborough.

During the Reformation period the divisions between the several chapels to the north and south of the nave were removed; and so since that date Chichester has been the only cathedral in England which has what may be called five aisles, and it is wider than any other, excepting York, being ninety-one feet across.

The central space, or nave proper, is divided into eight bays throughout its length. The vertical lines which mark these divisions are the triple attached vaulting shafts. They support the transverse ribs of the stone vault; and from their carved Purbeck marble capitals spring also the wall and diagonal ribs. A Purbeck string-course in each case separates the triforium gallery from the arcade below and from the clerestory above.

Photochrom Co., Ltd., photo.

THE NAVE, LOOKING EAST.

The nave arcades have round arches. The fine stone facing of the piers toward the nave, the small columns in the jambs, the vaulting shafts, and the moulded outer member of the arches are all additions to the twelfth-century structure. In the triforium, the round arch again occurs with two smaller sub-arches of similar shape. In the nave these were not altered after the second fire; but the clerestory above was much changed in character. The central arch of the three remained semicircular, but the side ones became pointed in place of the early round arches. The detached columns, the. jamb shafts, and the moulding of the arches were all altered in detail; and the stone used was of finer texture, like that with which the piers of the arcade below were faced.

S. B. Bolas & Co., photo.

THE SOUTH AISLE, FROM THE NAVE.

In the **South Aisle** there is a good view, which extends beyond the transept into the small chapel of S. Mary Magdalen at the east end, in which is the only really fine stained-glass window in the church. The chapel aisle to the south of this, again, is interesting, in that it still retains some signs of what purposes it served in former days. The two western bays were originally the **chapel of S. George**. Those to the east were dedicated as the **chapel of S. Clement**. In each of these the old piscina and aumbry remain near where the altar had been placed. The latter chapel has now been restored in memory of Bishop Durnford (see page 121). Mr. G.F. Bodley, A.R.A., and Mr. T. Garner were the architects who designed the new work. The old wall arcade is now again used as part of the reredos. The figures under the arches are—in the centre S. Clement, on the south S. Anselm, and on the north S. Alphege. In the quatrefoils above are figures of two angels bearing in their hands shields, on which are represented the symbols of the Passion. Behind the altar, which is of oak, is a white marble re-table. The deeply moulded arch which separates the two vaulted bays of each of these chapels is carried by some very beautiful carved capitals. Above them may be seen the square abaci which are so much used in all the later work in the cathedral. They are peculiarly a French characteristic, and serve to indicate the relationship there was between the English and Continental schools of mediæval architecture.

Beyond this chapel is the doorway from the south porch, which gives access to the west walk of the cloister.

The doorway on the right in the south aisle next to the entrance to the south arm of the transept leads to the **Bishop's Consistory Court** (or Langton's Chapter House), which is now a muniment-room.

The small chamber above the south porch is supposed to have been a secret **Treasury**. It is approached through the muniment-room, and has been popularly known as the "Lollard's Prison."

The **North Aisle** is similar to that on the south side. Towards its western end is the entrance door from the north porch.

The north chapel aisle was originally used as three separate chapels until the divisions between them were removed. The two bays at the west were the **chapel of S. Anne**; the two next east of this formed the chapel of the Four Virgins, and the last bay was the small chapel of SS. Thomas and Edmund. In the first named of these there may still be seen, in the jambs, the capitals, and the arch-moulds of the north-western window, some of the colour decoration of which so much remained until the nineteenth century. The space in the north wall shows where the aumbry used to be. The small remnants of the division wall at the east are some slight indication of what the design of the arcading on this wall was before it was destroyed. In the next chapel, that of the **Four Virgins**, there is nothing to show where the aumbry or the piscina was. But on the north 'the position of the arcading on the east dividing wall remains. The **chapel of SS. Thomas and Edmund** has an arcade on the east wall similar to that in the chapel of S. Clement. The aumbry is on the north and the piscina on the south side of the position which the altar used to occupy.

The **Rood-Screen** at the entrance to the choir from the nave was erected in 1889, and is a memorial of Archdeacon Walker. It was designed by Mr. T. Garner. At the point where the arms of the cross meet is a figure representing the "Agnus Dei," and at the extremities of the cross are carvings of the four-winged figures of the cherubim.

The **Pulpit** was designed by Sir Gilbert Scott, and is a memorial of Dean Hook. It is very elaborately carved, and is made of Caen stone and Purbeck marble. The four figures are intended to represent Matthew, Mark, Luke, and John.

The **Lectern** of brass was presented to the church as a memorial of Richard Owen, of Chichester, by his daughter.

The **Font** under the south-western tower is a copy of an old one in the church at Shoreham. It was the gift of Bishop Durnford, as a memorial of his wife.

The **Monuments in the Nave** have in many cases suffered from bad usage, and in most instances they do not now occupy their original places in the building.

The canopied memorial to Bishop Durnford (1),[30] under which is a recumbent effigy, forms part of the screen between S. Clement's chapel and the south aisle of the nave. It was designed by Mr. Garner. There are several tablets in the nave and aisles by Flaxman. The best are those to the memory of Captain Cromwell's wife and daughter (2), in S. Clement's chapel, and one on the north side of the nave, in the chapel of the Four Virgins, as a memorial of Collins (3), the poet, who was a native of Chichester. The two recumbent figures under the arch leading into this same chapel are said to be those of Richard Fitz-Alan, Earl of Arundel, and his wife (4). It was restored by Richardson. Fitz-Alan was beheaded in 1397. Some say that these two figures were removed from the chapel of the monastery of the Grey Friars at the time of the Reformation, and were placed in their present position in 1843, having been found embedded in the stonework of the chapel wall close by. The base upon which the figures rest is modern. The earl is represented in full armour. At his feet is a lion, and at his head, under the helmet, is a coronet and a lion's head. At the countess's feet is a dog, and her head rests upon two pillows.

The most beautiful monument now remaining in the church is that which is said to represent Maud, Countess of Arundel (1270) (5). The modelling of the whole figure and the long flowing lines of her robes are worthy of careful study. The whole pose and the disposition of the two angels at the head arranging the pillows, with the two dogs upon which her feet rest, have been finely conceived and well executed. The hands are clasped over the breast, with the forearms bent upwards slightly towards the face. On each of the long sides of the base supporting the figure are six elongated quatrefoil panels, containing in all six female figures and six shields. Between the quatrefoils are winged heads of ten angelic figures. The blazoning of the shields is entirely gone, and the brilliant colouring that once covered the entire monument is only to be traced in a few places. The outer robe still shows some signs of the rich blue with which it used to be covered. The face of the figure appears to be badly mutilated, but the damage to the features has been done principally by an endeavour to preserve them. A thick coat of plaster had been placed over the face to protect it from injury, perhaps in the seventeenth century or earlier, and this was never completely removed. It had become gradually polished like the material of the figure itself, and so it remains, with a cut across it to represent a mouth. The remains of the real face are still hidden beneath.

[30] The figures in parenthesis refer to the numbers on the plan at the end.

S. B. Bolas & Co., photo.

THE SACRISTY.

Close to this effigy, but in the aisle farther to the east, and on the north wall, are two admirable memorial tablets which were designed in the eighteenth century. One is in memory of Dean Hayley and his wife (6), and the other in memory of Henry Baker and his wife and their only child (7), who, by comparison with the other tablet, appears to have been a second wife of the same Thomas Hayley.

Close to the porch in the south aisle is the only complete old brass in the building (8). It is dated 1592, and records the fact that "Mr. William Bradbridge" was "thrice Maior of this Cittie," and "had vi sonnes & viii daughters." The other monuments in the nave are those of Matthew Quantock, Dean Cloos, Bishop Arundel, and William Huskisson, sometime member of Parliament for Chichester. One on the south side of the west porch is Bishop Stephen de Berghstead's, and the other opposite on the north is a work of the fifteenth century.

The **Choir and Sanctuary**—These are very different in appearance now from what they were, as will be seen by reference to the chapter on the history of the fabric.

The **Reredos** was designed by Messrs. Slater & Carpenter, and has never been completed. It is generally considered that it is not at all in keeping with the character of the building, and there is some hope that it may be one day removed. The subject of the figure-work in the panel is "The Ascension."

THE ALTAR AND REREDOS.

The **Altar** was presented by the late Mr. J.F. France, and is made of oak. Some of the frontals are very elaborate examples of modern embroidery.

The **Pavements** are composed of many specimens of various coloured marbles.

The **Stalls** are those which have been in use since the fourteenth century. All the furniture of the choir had been removed for safety before the fall of the tower and spire: but the bishop's throne (9) and the stalls for the dean and precentor have been added since that time.

The **Candelabrum** which hangs from the vault was presented by Lady Featherstonhaugh and two other ladies, in the eighteenth century.

The **Iron Grilles** which screen the eastern part of the choir from the aisles are good examples of simple modern ironwork copied from old examples; they were made in Chichester by Halsted & Sons.

The **Organ** was placed on the north side of the choir after it had been removed from its earlier position on the Arundel screen; and in 1888, when it was largely remodelled, a new oak case was designed for it. It was made originally by Harris in 1678, and had then only one manual and no pedals; but between this date and the last alteration, it had already been enlarged no less than at six different times.

As the choir stalls are immediately under the crossing, above which rises the new central tower and spire, they are a convenient place from which to examine the work of restoration. The new work represents as nearly as possible all that was there before the collapse of the old piers and arches.

In the **South Transept** the most important feature is the beautifully designed stonework of the tracery in the south window; but this may be seen better from the cloisters, as the crude vulgarity of the bad painted glass makes it difficult to examine it from within the building.

The **Sacristy** (10), now used as a choir school and vestry, is a large vaulted chamber, lighted on the south side by six small windows (see page 87).

The **Chapel of S. Pantaleon** (11), on the east side of the transept, still retains the old piscina in the south wall; but it is used now as the vestry for the dean and canons.

The vaulting ribs in the part of the transept between this chapel and the sacristy are carved like those in the last bay of the presbytery next to the lady-chapel, and are of the same date. They appear to be part of the work done during Bishop Gilbert Leophardo's episcopate.

The **Pictures** by Bernardi on the back of the choir stalls (see illustration, p. 113) represent Ceadwalla and Henry VIII. granting and confirming privileges to the bishops of their day. The portraits of the bishops of the see from Wilfrid to Sherborne are in the north transept.

S. B. Bolas & Co., photo.

THE TRIFORIUM IN THE CHOIR.

The **South Aisle of the Choir** is entered from the south transept under a deeply moulded arch. On the south is the priest-vicars' vestry (12), and at the east end the **chapel of S. Mary Magdalen**. This chapel was restored by Messrs. G.F. Bodley, A.R.A., and T. Garner, architects, in memory of the Rev. T.F. Crosse, who was precentor and canon of the cathedral. The aumbry in the north wall was the receptacle in which S. Richard's head was preserved in a case of silver. This is mentioned in William de Tenne's will. On the other side is the old piscina. The paintings in the panels by Miss Lowndes represent, on the north side (i) S. Richard celebrating the Eucharist in S. Edmund's Chapel, (ii) the same bishop preaching, and (iii) his death; on the south, (i) Mary anoints our Lord's Feet, (ii) The Crucifixion, (iii) After the Resurrection. The carved and painted reredos is of stone. Close to this chapel is the doorway into the church from the east walk of the cloisters; in the spandrels of the arches, both inside and outside, are the arms of William of Wykeham. Above it is a window, the glass in which was given by Cardinal Manning (when Archdeacon of Chichester) in memory of his wife.

H.C. Corlette, delin.

DECORATION ON THE VAULT OF THE LADY-CHAPEL, BY TH. BERNARDI, 1519.

(Scale about 4 feet 10 ins. to 1 in).

The **Presbytery**, Ambulatory, or retro-choir, is the space between the back of the reredos and the entrance to the lady-chapel. The design in detail of these two bays is very different in character from the three in the choir, which are like those in the nave. The two piers of Purbeck marble are circular, and about them are grouped four detached shafts of the same material. They are united only at the base and by the abacus above the capitals, which are beautifully carved (see page 16). The main arches in the two bays are not pointed, but round, like those in the nave and choir; but, unlike the latter, they have deeply cut mouldings in three orders. The triforium arcade above, on the north and south sides, has moulded and carved details of a similar character. Some of the beautifully carved figure-work still remains in the spandrels between the subsidiary pointed arches. But the most beautiful piece of design in all this work is in the arches of the triforium passage across the east wall, above the entrance to the lady-chapel.

THE PRESBYTERY, OR RETRO-CHOIR, LOOKING NORTH-EAST.

It should be noticed that the sub-arches in the triforium here are pointed, not round, as in the case of those in the same position westward of this portion. And the support to these arches in the centre, is a group of shafts instead of only one column. The clerestory, however, offers a greater contrast to the earlier work in that the central arch, as well as the side ones, is lifted up much higher, the detached columns being lengthened to obtain the alteration. Each arch also, at this level, is now pointed.

S. Richard's shrine occupied the bay in the presbytery immediately behind the High Altar. It stood upon a platform which was approached on its eastern side by steps, and was enclosed by iron grilles. The platform was removed at the time of the general restoration in 1861-1867, and upon it used to stand also the tombs of Bishop Day and Bishop Christopherson or Curteys.

THE LADY-CHAPEL.

The **Lady-Chapel**, as its walls and vaulting clearly show, was once completely decorated with designs in colour. The windows now are the only parts that indicate an attempt to renew this portion of its earlier condition. The new reredos is of alabaster, and was designed by Messrs Carpenter & Ingelow.

S. B. Bolas & Co., photo.

THE NORTH CHOIR-AISLE, LOOKING WEST.

The **North Choir Aisle** contains some monuments which are referred to separately. The now unused chapel at its eastern end was dedicated to S. Catharine.

The **Library** is approached through a doorway in this aisle. There is a chamber above in which was the library of pre-Reformation days. The present library formed the chapel of S. John the Baptist and S. Edmund the King (13) until it became the chancel of the parish church of S. Peter the Great, the north transept being used as its nave. Part of the vaulting in it is unlike any other in the building, having the chevron or zigzag ornament cut on the side of the mouldings of the ribs (see page 98).

The library collection contains many relics of various kinds: among them are Oslac's grant of land to the church at Selsea, A.D. 780; a manuscript of the twelfth century; Cranmer's copy of the "Consultatio" of Herman of Cologne; an old Sarum missal; the sealed book of Charles II.; fragments of ecclesiastical vessels; and a leaden "Absolution" of Bishop Godfrey dating from the eleventh century.

The **North Transept** has on its west side two of the old twelfth-century round-arched windows, and opposite are the two large round-arched openings into the library and the chamber above it. The vaulting of this transept is not the same in detail as that to the south of the choir, and is rather earlier in the type of its mouldings. Close by the south springing of the arch leading to the library is one of the few pieces of figure-carving in the church. It is a head full of vigour and character.

The **Monuments in the Transepts and Choir** have been injured and restored or removed at various times. The large one (14) under the south window is Langton's tomb and effigy (d. 1336). The new one nearest to the singing school is a memorial and effigy of Mr. John Abel Smith, of Dale Park, who represented Chichester in the House of Commons. On the east wall is another tomb of Tudor date (15), with niches for sculpture. The tomb next to the back of the choir-stalls (16) is that of Bishop Richard de la Wych. The two panels in relief (17), in the south aisle of the choir are works of about the twelfth century (see page 105). It is supposed that originally they were brought to Chichester from Selsea. They were discovered in 1829 hidden in the wall behind the woodwork of the stalls in the choir, and were subsequently placed in their present position. The subject of the one nearest to the transept is the "Raising of Lazarus," and of the other, "Our Lord with Mary and Martha at Bethany." These are two of the most interesting relics of earlier days that remain in the cathedral. Historically and artistically, they are of much value, but at present no more than has been stated is known about them. Bishop Sherborne's monument (18) was built during his lifetime, and at his death he provided for its care by New College, of which he had been a fellow. It is still well cared for; but with its original decorations it must have been a very beautiful object.

Dean Hook, who died in 1875, is commemorated by a monument (19) opposite Sherborne's. It was designed by Sir Gilbert Scott, and, like the pavements of the choir, it has in its composition many specimens of coloured marbles. Much of the detail is executed in mosaic. Under the arch of the presbytery arcade nearest to the reredos, on the south side, is Bishop Day's tomb (20). On the south side of the lady-chapel, close to the entrance, are the memorial slabs of two early bishops, perhaps Hilary and John de Greneford, beneath the arch where Bishop Gilbert's effigy was placed. On the opposite side is a space under an arch in which may be traced the lines of some decoration which once ornamented some memorial. Upon the floor below is the memorial of Bishop Ralph (21), the builder of the first portions of the cathedral. Close by is a large wall tablet in memory of Bishop Thomas Bickley. It is a design of the seventeenth-century period, and is interesting of its kind. Under the arch on the north side of the presbytery, opposite Day's tomb, is that of Bishop Christopherson or Curteys (22), and against the wall of the aisle near the chapel of S. Catharine is a curious marble slab with some carving upon it. It represents two hands, with parts of the arms, supporting a heart, and the full inscription, now almost gone, was "ICY GIST LE COEUR DE MAUDDE" ("Here lies the heart of Maud"). It is evidently work of an early date, but nothing is accurately known of its history, though it has been assumed that it was made in the twelfth or thirteenth century (23). To the west of this is a bust of Bishop Otter (24). In an arched recess in the wall nearer to the library is the tomb and effigy of Bishop Storey (25). Close to this are two memorials of the sixteenth century. On the west side of the north transept are the monuments of Bishops Henry King, Carleton, and Grove.

S. B. Bolas & Co., photo.

THE LIBRARY.

The **Stained Glass** in the cathedral is all modern, and most of it is of the worst possible kind. It is bad in design and crude in colour, and much of it is not really stained glass at all, but a painted substitute. The only really good window in the building is that at the east end of the south choir aisle in S. Mary Magdalen's chapel. It was designed by Mr. C.E. Kempe. The glass in the lady-chapel windows is better than most of the rest, and it is admitted that the worst glass that was ever placed in any cathedral church by a generous munificence is that which is now in the large window of the south transept.

Photochrom Co., Ltd., photo.

THE TOWN CROSS.
Built by Bishop Storey, c. 1500.

CHAPTER IV.

THE DIOCESE AND SEE: OTHER BUILDINGS IN THE CITY.

To trace the history of the establishment of the city of Chichester we need go back to the time when the Romans had occupied the same site under the ancient name of Regnum. They had fortified themselves in this position, and evidence of their occupation is to be found to-day in the subdivision of the city into four parts by those streets which meet at the Market Cross. But as the centre of the Imperial fabric became weaker the dependencies were abandoned, and the Roman legions recalled early in the fifth century. So when in 477 A.D. "came Aelle to Britain, and his three sons, Cymen, Wlencing, and Cissa, with three ships," and landed at "the place which is named Cymenesora, and there slew many Welsh, and drove some into the forest which is named Andredslea," there were no Roman soldiers to oppose them.

In this brief sentence, quoted from the Anglo-Saxon chronicle, there is a reference to several interesting matters which concern the later history of the South Saxons, their acceptance of Christianity, and the foundation of that Church—first at Selsea, then at Chichester—which was to be the future local centre to support and foster the faith they for so long rejected. The Jute leaders, Hengest and Horsa, had established themselves on British soil in 449 A.D. This was twenty-eight years before Aelle arrived, and with his followers "slew many Welsh"; that is, the British natives, the Wealas, or strangers, whom he found in possession of the land. The place "named Cymenesora," at which Aelle had landed, was close to Wittering, at the mouth of Chichester harbour. And the chronicle, relating what had occurred thirteen years later, records how "in this year (490-1) Aelle and Cissa besieged Andredes ceaster, and slew all that dwelt therein, so that not even one Briton was left." This fortress of Anderida, which had been a Roman *castrum*, occupied the spot now called Pevensey, the landing-place of a later conqueror, the Norman William, in 1066. It guarded on the east the strip of land between the South Downs and the sea; and when it fell before them, the Saxons became masters of the region to the north known then as Andredeslea, or Andredeswold, the forest or weald of Anderida. To the west was Regnum, Cissa's Ceaster, or Chichester, another of those fortresses which the provident and energetic Romans had established along the South Coast.

One of Aelle's followers, named Boso, or Bosa, settled at the head of a branch of Chichester harbour, and, as in the case of his superior, Cymen, the place was named after him, as Bosenham, or Bosham. This was in the fifth century. Augustine began his work in Kent late in the sixth century, and Birinus, who was sent independently direct from Rome, had undertaken the conversion of the West Saxons fifteen years before the middle of the succeeding century. But neither by these missionaries nor their brethren was the territory of the South Saxons affected.

The West Saxons, by conquest, extended their rule westward and northward, and missionary enterprise followed the course of military success and subsequent civil protection. The original British occupiers of the land withdrew to Wales, or else became subject to the conquerors. Similar had been the course of events which followed the taking of Kent by the Jutes. So when Augustine arrived he was welcomed by Aethelberht, whose wife Bertha, a Frankish princess, was already a Christian.

Augustine having founded the see of Canterbury, was soon enabled, by the help of political and social influence, to effect the establishment of other sees. Rochester, London, and York were soon centres of activity; but these neighbour principalities had not, ecclesiastically, affected the territories that were close to their respective domains; for the kingdom of the South Saxons remained, nearly two centuries after Aelle's conquest, in the same heathen condition as prevailed in his day.

Bede relates that at Bosham, Dicul had founded a monastery where, "surrounded by woods and water, lived five or six brethren, serving the Lord in humility and poverty." But "no one cared to emulate their life, or listen to their teaching." Dicul came from Ireland, and it is supposed that he had been educated in the monastic centre of missionary life which in the sixth century had been founded there. It is not, however, known how these few men found their way to the South Saxon shores, and their presence there had no influence upon the minds of those invaders who had possessed themselves of the adjacent lands. A quarrel in the Northumbrian kingdom was the cause which sent a missionary to Sussex in 680 A.D.

Ecgfrith and his witan had banished **Wilfrith**, Archbishop of York, from his see. The unfortunate exile wandered some time in search of welcome. Eventually he found his way to Sussex, where Aethelwealh and his Christian wife offered him a new field for his energies. Twenty years earlier he had been in the same kingdom. On that occasion, having been consecrated by the Bishop of Paris, he was returning from Gaul when the vessel in which he travelled was driven upon the coast and stranded. While in this helpless condition they were discovered and attacked by the South Saxons, who were three times beaten off, but whilst they were continuing their preparations for another assault, the vessel rose with the tide and escaped. Under other circumstances he was now among these people again. The famine which prevailed at the time of his arrival gave him the necessary opportunity to gain their affections by first satisfying their material needs. He showed the starving folk how to catch fish with nets which he and his companions had made, and then was able to teach them other things. He preached with success for some time, and baptized many who heard him. Bede has left a record characteristic of his day, in which he relates that immediately they had accepted the faith which he taught, "the rain, so long withheld, revisited the thirsty land."

Aethelwealh, grateful for Wilfrith's aid, granted him lands at Selsea. The bishop at once gave freedom to those families and their slaves who occupied the district, and baptized them, giving them release, as Bede has told, from spiritual and temporal bond's at the same time. Selsea thus became another see from which Christian principle and practice might be taught in the midst of the surrounding tribes. In this spot, near the residence of the king, a church was built, in which the bishop's cathedra was placed. The structure was dedicated to S. Peter, and was the first cathedral church in Sussex. It is not now known what the architectural character of this building was. Perhaps there was some attempt in its design to take advantage of such suggestions as the Romans left behind them at Regnum, for we find in early instances of English architecture that such examples had exercised some influence upon the elementary efforts of those days. But it is more likely that his first church was nothing but a small and simple barn, for men were not then burdened with the idea that a cathedral must be a big church, provided it served as a centre from which the bishop could use his pastoral responsibility. During Wilfrith's stay at Selsea many changes took place.

Then Ceadwalla, who had defeated Aedilwalch, or Aethelwealh, confirmed the grants to the Church made by his predecessor, in return for the kindness he had received from Wilfrith some time before.

Under their new head the missionaries at Selsea undertook, with the king's sanction, to convert those who inhabited the neighbouring island of Wight and also parts of the mainland which now were subject to the new ruler. But after five years in the south Wilfrith returned to his old diocese of York. Sussex, to a large extent, had accepted the faith he endeavoured to teach, and many churches were established and organised before his departure.

For some years after Wilfrith had returned to York there was no bishop in charge of the newly founded diocese in Sussex. The community of workers he had brought together at Selsea still continued to exist; but Sussex in ecclesiastical affairs was subject to Winchester during this interval. Ceadwalla, when Kentwine, King of Wessex, died in 685, had begun "to strive for the kingdom," so the chronicle has recorded, and having established himself upon the throne, he succeeded also in conquering the ruler of Sussex, and so brought both kingdoms under his sway. Wilfrith had converted him to the Christian faith; but when this prelate was recalled to his former diocese, no one had been appointed to carry on the work he had begun. For twenty years this vacancy continued. Then, after the death of Ceadwalla, Ine, his successor, divided the large diocese, which was subject to the Bishop of Winchester, by making, with the consent of his witan, a new see at Sherburne and reviving that of Selsea. Of this latter, **Eadberht** was appointed the first bishop in the year 709. The community in Selsea over which Eadberht had presided before his consecration was a secular foundation. Whatever was the principle upon which it had been founded, there seems no doubt that during the interim which elapsed before a bishop was placed in charge some elementary form of government was carried on by a succession of elected presidents. This body was either composed of secular clergy, who were distributed throughout the diocese, living as priests in charge of parishes *in sæculo,* or it was a foundation supported by those who lived according to a *regula.* The regulars were those who lived together, having vowed obedience to some particular form of rule. These were unmarried men, who used one building, property, refectory, and dormitory of the institution in common. Not all of these were ordained, as there were among them lay brothers as well as those who were priests. But the seculars—those in the world—were not subject to rules and conditions such as these. Many, as priests living in their parishes, were married men.

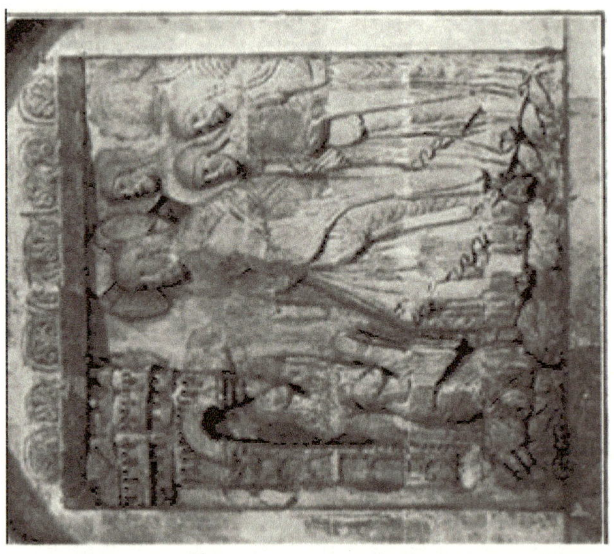

Our Lord with Martha and Mary.

The Raising of Lazarus.

SCULPTURED PANELS IN THE SOUTH CHOIR-AISLE, SUP-
POSED TO HAVE BEEN BROUGHT FROM THE CATHEDRAL AT
SELSEA.

After the consecration of Eadberht and his installation as Bishop of Selsea, the cathedra, or episcopal chair, was occupied successively by twenty prelates. The period during which these held office, including the few intervals when for a time the see remained vacant, extended over about three hundred and seventy years. Little is known of these bishops further than that their signatures are to be found attached to various charters. These were all called Bishops of the South Saxons.

Aethelgar was Bishop of Selsea in 980. He had been a member of the monastic colony at Glastonbury, near Wells. After occupying the see for about eight years, he succeeded Dunstan as Archbishop of Canterbury.

Bishops **Ordberht** and **Aelmer** were bishops after Aethelgar; and then the next prelate of importance was **Aethelric**, who was a Benedictine of Christ Church, Canterbury. He was learned in the ancient laws and customs of his country, and when a very old man acted as one of the arbitrators appointed to settle the differences which had arisen between Lanfranc and Odo, Earl of Kent. Aethelric had been consecrated by Stigand, Archbishop of Canterbury, who was removed from the Primacy by William the Conqueror to make room for Lanfranc, his own nominee.

The see of Selsea was governed by three other bishops till William appointed one of his chaplains to the office. This was **Stigand** (1070-1087), but not that Stigand (the Primate) who at the same royal bidding had to make room for Lanfranc. It was while he was still an occupant of the see that the transfer to Chichester was effected. He earned the displeasure of the king by refusing to consecrate Gausbert to the Abbey of Battle unless the monk would come to Chichester for the ceremony. He had some trouble, too, with his metropolitan, Lanfranc, on account of a dispute concerning the limits of his jurisdiction. Certain parishes within the territory of his diocese were claimed as subject to the more eastern see. The Primate established his right to these "peculiars," and the right obtained until the last century, when all such holdings were abolished by law.

Godfrey (1087-1088) evidently incurred the displeasure of his papal superior, as the only known record of his very brief episcopate is represented by a discovery which was made in 1830 when an absolution from the Pope, inscribed upon a leaden cross, was dug up in the paradise close to the south choir aisle.

It was not till three years had elapsed since Godfrey's death that **Ralph de Luffa** (1091-1123) was consecrated to the vacancy by Thomas, Archbishop of York. Meanwhile the king enjoyed the temporalities of the see. In his person we meet a figure of much importance to the history of the fabric and see, for to his energy and initiative we owe the greater part of the cathedral building that remains to-day.

Ralph's activity was not wholly absorbed by his interest in the architectural idea which he hoped to realise. He spent much time and care attending to the needs of the churches of which he was the overseer. He visited them regularly three times in the year for the purpose of effecting reforms when they were necessary, for teaching, and for developing the organisation of the diocese as it was affected by the condition of each parochial unit. Thus by his office and oversight he was endeavouring to maintain the necessary relations between the particular churches and their cathedral centre. In defence of these same members of the local and general ecclesiastical body he was obliged to resent the attempted interference of two kings of the realm. Henry I. wished to fill his pockets by imposing fines upon the clergy. To oppose this the bishop closed all the churches in the diocese and blocked up the entrances with thorns; and so, except in the monasteries, the offering of public worship ceased. The restriction was in time removed, and the king acknowledged the bishop's plea that he should endeavour to replenish the coffers of his poor see, so that the injured cathedral might be repaired, rather than reduce it to poverty by extortion.

Ralph is credited with having established the office of "dean"[31] at Chichester—the first of the four cathedral dignitaries, of which the others are the præcentor, the chancellor, and the treasurer.

Seffrid Pelochin, or **d'Escures** (1125-1147), ceded to the king's aggression the rights and privileges Ralph had gained. He was obliged to vacate the see in 1145, [an]d returned to Glastonbury, where he had been abbot before he was made bishop. His name figures in the list which Roger of Hoveden gives in his chronicle, as one among the bishops who were at the Council of London in 1129.

Hilary (1147-1169) was a bishop who was before all things an ecclesiastic. To Ralph Luffa's foundation of the dean's office he added those of the chancellor and treasurer, if not also, as is supposed, that of the præcentor. With Hilary began the traditional post of confessor to the queen of the realm. Stephen had given him this office, and at the same time added to the privilege a perpetual chaplaincy in connection with the castle at Pevensey.

The letters from Popes Eugenius and Alexander III., which confirmed the possessions held by the see and guaranteed a papal protection of the church in Chichester, are among the collection in the cathedral library. The properties these deeds acknowledge include that portion of the city—one fourth—in which the close was situated; and within this area were comprised the church itself, the episcopal palace, and the residences of the canons. The original grant of this land was made by William, Earl of Arundel, in 1147, who bestowed it among other things as compensation "for the damages which I once did to the same church." Hilary was Bishop of Chichester during that historic period when Becket opposed Henry II. He attempted, like the rest of the bishops, to heal the breach; and Tennyson, in "Becket," adopting a phrase he used, makes him say to his Primate, "Hath not thine ambition set the Church this day between the hammer and the anvil ... fealty to the King, obedience to thyself?" He went to Sens, to plead as an advocate on the king's behalf before Pope Alexander III. and the French king. The result of this meeting was that England was placed under the ban of excommunication. But Henry replied by declaring that the property of all who acted upon it should be confiscated and themselves banished. The bishop was involved also in a local contest with the Abbot of Battle, who refused to consider himself subject to his episcopal jurisdiction.

After Hilary's death in 1169 the revenues of the see were for four years ap-

---

[31] Stephens, p. 49.

propriated to his own uses by the king, who late in the year 1173 appointed **John Greenford** (1174-1180), who was Dean of Chichester, to the vacancy. The bishop-elect was not consecrated until, in 1174, he, with three more nominated about the same time, had done penance before Becket's tomb at Canterbury. Little is known of him except that he attended some ecclesiastical councils.

The episcopate of **Seffrid II.** (1180-1204) introduces an important period of activity, during which great alterations were made in the fabric of the cathedral.

Simon Fitz Robert, or **Simon of Wells** (1204-1207), was a bishop whose favour with the king (John) enabled him to do much for the see. He had held a post in the Royal Exchequer, and had been guardian of the Fleet Prison as well as Provost of Beverley and Archdeacon of Wells. The benefactions he obtained were various. A charter was granted by which the see should hold its property free from impost, under the protection of the king. The bishop, with his dean and chapter, were practically exempted from the jurisdiction of the local civil courts and from the payment of customs and tolls within the same sphere. Within the bounds of the property owned by the see they were to rule without restraint, and in the presence of a royal official "the view of Frank Pledge was to be held in the bishop's court." In the patent rolls of King John there are two entries, dated 1205 A.D. and 1206 A.D., by which the bishop was granted permission to take Purbeck marble for the repair of his church without hindrance, from the coast of Dorset to Chichester.[32] But precautions were taken to prevent any of the material thus obtained from being used elsewhere. A further grant, the evidence of which is now removed, allowed the chapter to build premises beyond the precincts northward, which encroached twelve feet into the roadway now known as West Street. A row of lime-trees now stands where these houses remained till the middle of the last century. For six years after Simon's death John kept the see vacant, and during the interim enjoyed the temporalities.

Richard Poore was then consecrated bishop in 1215. He had been Dean of Old Sarum. But after occupying the see for no more than two years, he was translated to Salisbury.

Ranulf of Warham (1217-1224) bequeathed some property to the see[33]; but otherwise he did little, except as a fortunate collector of cattle, for the support of which his successor provided pasturage.

Ralph Neville (1224-1244) was a bishop of more than local celebrity. Like Langton, the archbishop, he withstood the demands which the papacy and Henry III. made in their endeavours to impoverish the Church in England. For this opposition the king removed him temporarily from the post of Chancellor of the Realm, a position he held from 1226 to 1240. His "fame rests more upon his repute as a statesman faithful in many perils, and a singular pillar of truth in the affairs of the kingdom."[34] He succeeded in procuring the payment to the Church of tithe from some royal properties which had been withheld, and left provision for the supply

[32] See Walcott, p. 15, note c, May 24th, 1207.
[33] Stephens, p. 57.
[34] Matt. Paris.

of twelve quarters of wheat annually to the poor in Chichester. Some, notes preserved in the cathedral records lead to the supposition that the portion of the old central tower above the roof and up to the parapet at the foot of the spire was built, or at least begun, during Ralph's tenure of the see. One of these memoranda shows that he released from twenty days' penance those who should visit the cathedral and contribute to the maintenance of the fabric. The others state that he expended one hundred and thirty marks upon repairs, and his executors paid over one hundred and forty marks to the dean and chapter for the purpose of finishing a stone tower which it had been found necessary to repair.[35] Three years after his death it was nearly completed. Bishop Neville died at his house by Chancellor's Lane, now Chancery Lane. His property later passed into the hands of the Earl of Lincoln, and was known then as the inn, or hospital, of Lincoln. The estate is now covered by the buildings of Lincoln's Inn,[36] and that portion which is still the property of the see is known as "The Chichester Rents."

Ralph's successor was Richard of Wych (1245-1253), generally called St. Richard. He had studied under Edmund and Grosseteste at Oxford, and also in Paris and Bologna. Returning from Europe, he became Chancellor of the University of Oxford, then of the diocese of Canterbury. Having withdrawn again to France, he was ordained priest at Orleans, and then worked as vicar at Deal, from which post he was called upon to occupy again his earlier office at Canterbury. Then came his appointment to Chichester. The canons had elected Robert Passelew, but the archbishop objected. Henry III., having supported the first nominee, disputed Richard's election. Meanwhile the king appropriated the temporalities for two years. Richard appealed to Innocent IV., who confirmed the appointment and consecrated Richard at Lyons in 1245. This did not end the difference, for on the new bishop's return he was obliged to accept the hospitality of his clergy, the king being still hostile. But he did not allow these difficulties to interfere with his attention to episcopal duty, for he walked throughout the diocese, organising and teaching as he went. In his leisure he followed the pursuits of his youth, and spent his spare time in farming and gardening. He was an excellent man, whose peculiar sanctity rests largely upon his having succeeded in doing the duties some of his predecessors had disregarded, and for a generosity which outran his income. Accepting that law which the papacy had added to those of Christianity, he treated the married clergy with the severity his sense of duty and obedience urged, for he deprived them of their benefices, and their wives were denied the offices of the Church both before and after death. Any bequests to them by their husbands, he declared, should be confiscated, and the funds derived by this means devoted to the needs of the cathedral building Rather inconsistently he taught the beneficed clergy that they should use hospitality and charity; but like another Malachi, he reminded men that to withhold the tithe of their increase from the Church made them robbers not of the clergy, but of their Creator. He instituted the fund afterwards known as "S. Richard's Pence." It was a system by which regular offerings should be made for the completion and maintenance of the cathedral fabric. And, characteristically, he obtained the support of the archbishop and seven other prel-

[35] See Walcott, p. 15, note c.
[36] See Stephens, p. 61, cf. Murray's "Chichester."

ates in their approval of his wish that they should "recommend visits and offerings to Chichester, for the repair and completion of the cathedral." This is another evidence of the great extent of those building operations that were in progress throughout the thirteenth century. Just before his death he began to preach a crusade, but died at Dover. In his will he still remembered the cathedral by leaving a legacy of forty pounds for the needs of the fabric.

John of Clymping (1253-1262) succeeded Richard. His episcopate appears chiefly remarkable for the growth of stories about the miraculous powers and saintly life of his predecessor.

Stephen of Berghsted (1262-1288) now occupied the see. During his episcopate Richard was canonised, a deputation, sent at great cost to Rome, having succeeded in persuading Urban IV. that his merits and fame deserved an honour which should bring wealth and celebrity to the see in whose cathedral his body was laid; so in 1276 the remains of his body were removed from their tomb and placed at the back of the high altar in a shrine, or feretory, dedicated to him.

Gilbert de Sancto Leophardo (1288-1305) was a bishop who, like S. Richard, devoted himself to his diocesan duties with a singleminded purpose which was not a common virtue with all mediæval prelates. He endeavoured to regulate the habits of those clergy who accepted their privileges but were inclined to neglect the duties and responsibilities these involved. His interest in the fabric of the cathedral was expressed principally by the additions that were made to the lady-chapel during his episcopate.

John Langton (1305-1337) took a conspicuous part in the suppression of the knights templars during the reign of Edward II. in obedience to the papal order regarding them. He was Chancellor of the Realm before his elevation to the episcopate, and showed his energy as a statesman locally by commanding the restoration of rights to some vicars of the cathedral who had been suspended in accordance with the provisions of certain statutes which the dean and chapter made without his consent. Like Bishop Gilbert, he was an instrument by whose sanction more changes were made in the building.

Robert of Stratford (1337-1362), another statesman bishop, succeeded Langton. He had also been chancellor, and asserted his episcopal authority as sternly as his predecessor.

Of **William of Lynn** (1362-1368) and his episcopacy little record remains; but

William Rede (1369-1385) earned some repute as a scholar, and was the founder of Merton College Library in Oxford, and it is to him that the diocese is indebted for the preservation of the early records relating to the see. Nothing of importance is known of the next three bishops:

Thomas Rushoke (1385-1389).

Richard Metford (1389-1395).

Robert Waldby (1395-1396).

TOMB ASSIGNED TO BISHOP RICHARD OF WYCH, AND PIC-
TURES ORIGINALLY BY BERNARDI.

Robert Rede (1397-1415), whose register is the earliest among those that remain, occupied the see during the reign of Henry IV. This record contains many interesting details concerning the part its compiler took in the endeavour to suppress the doctrines of Wycliffe and the Lollards; and it also shows that much disorder prevailed among the canons and vicars of the cathedral. One of the canons, besides stealing money from the treasury, appropriated for his private use some materials which had been intended for the repair of the church. Rectors of parishes allowed their cures to fall into a state of destitution, and left them to the care of poorly paid vicars while they themselves resided elsewhere. The see was not filled for two years after the death of Rede. Then followed in succession:

Stephen Patryngton (1417).

Henry Ware (1418).

John Kemp (1421).

Thomas Poldon (1421).

John Rickingale (1426).

Simon Sydenham (1429).

No registers remain relating to the affairs of the episcopate during the twenty years covered by their occupation of the see.

In the register left by **Richard Praty** (1438-1446) there is evidence that many of the negligences censured by Bishop Rede were still without correction. The discipline of the monastic houses in Sussex is represented as having become very lax.

Adam Moleyns, or **Molyneux** (1446-1450), was instrumental in arranging the marriage of Henry VI. with Margaret of Anjou. Many concessions were granted to him by the king for the benefit of himself and the diocese, but having become unpopular he was murdered by some sailors in Portsmouth early in 1450 when on his way to France.

Reginald Pecock (1450-1459), "being convicted of heresy, he resigned his bishopric," so say the records of the cathedral.

John Arundel (1459-1478). The record of his episcopal administration has been lost; but it is known that he built the screen named after him. He appears, however, to have been much less restless than his predecessor.

Edward Storey (1478-1503) has left in his register full accounts of his deeds and the condition of the diocese. It shows the latter had again become very disordered. Both the regular and secular bodies are charged with abusing the trust committed to them. Bishop Storey tried to correct this state of things. He proved his usefulness, otherwise, by the foundation of the Prebendal, or Free Grammar-School, in Chichester, and also by giving the Market Cross to the city for the benefit of the poor.

Of **Richard Fitz-James** (1503-1508) and his administration there is but little information.

With **Robert Sherburne** (1508-1536) we come to the close of a long period of ecclesiastical history—one during which the distinctly Christian, as opposed to the pagan, principles and forms of art had been developed. As bishop at Chichester he represented the Church and those principles which then in the west were taught in her name. Accordingly he protested against "the King's most dreadful commandment concerning (with other things) the uniting of the Supreme head of the Church of [? in] England with the Imperial Crown of this realm; and also the abolishing and secluding out of this realm the enormities and abuses of the Bishop of Rome's authority, usurped within the same." He wrote thus in 1534 to Cromwell. And obeying this command from the civil authority, he caused these orders to be published throughout the diocese. As a subject he obeyed his king; but, being honest, he could not as a bishop and a man disregard his principles when he found such obedience involved their denial. Consequently he resigned the see in 1536.

Richard Sampson (1536-1543) took part in the Reformation movement. Although he had defended the principle that the king was to be considered "high governor under God, and Supreme head of the Church of England," his principles appear to have been easily affected by the political weather that prevailed. His attitude in favour of every principle involved in the acceptance of the papacy appears in the support he gave to doctrines which had been rejected by the party of reform. He no doubt feared the results that might follow upon another attempt to adapt the Church's constitution to changed conditions.

In the time of **George Daye** (1543-1552) the pendulum moved again across the face of the political and ecclesiastical clock. He was a man whose convictions led him to support those same six articles which had been upheld by Bishop Sampson; and he attempted to prevent the introduction of the first prayer-book of Edward VI. in 1549, as well as the destruction of the earlier service-books in the following year. He was a man to be respected, for in the face of general opposition he proved that his convictions on important affairs were not ready to change at the sudden bidding of a new authority which he was unable to recognise. As he was not to be persuaded that his position was wrong, he was removed from the see towards the end of the year 1551. But we meet him again presently, for Bishop **John Scory** (1552-1554), who took his place, retired soon after Mary's accession. Bishop Daye came back to favour, preached at the coronation, reoccupied the see, and was now "a mighty busy man."[37] He caused some recent orders to be reversed by reviving the use of the earlier forms of liturgy, restoring the older ceremonial, and again setting up those altars in the churches which should never have been broken down. In his own words Daye "styeked" not at things trivial; but he would not assent to the abolition of essentials, however much they had been misused or become offensive in the eyes of untutored civil dignitaries and their party followers. Daye on his restoration had attempted to remove reformers and their opinions from the diocese by the aid of faggots and flames. But **John Christopherson** (1557-1559) was more energetic in upholding his authority and ideas by this same means; for Mary, though she would revive the papal supremacy, yet retained in her own hands the ecclesiastical position which the Throne in England had already assumed.

At the close of Mary's reign Bishop Christopherson died, and in his place Eliz-

____

[37] Strype, quoted by Dean Stephens, p. 190.

abeth put **William Barlow** (1559-1568), who had been removed from the see of Bath and Wells by her predecessor. He made some attempt to remove a variety of irregularities which had been introduced since the death of Sherburne, for the services of the Church had become much disordered in consequence of the many changes of attitude which had been favoured by the rulers, both civil and ecclesiastical, during nearly thirty years. Barlow's endeavour to bring this chaos to a new order was in accord with the methods of those who sought reform. He tried to carry out the injunction of Parker, the Primate, whose aim was to "reduce all to a Godly uniformitie." But any desire for unity in diversity was not likely to be satisfied unless it was sought for with at least some unanimity of hope and aim. After his death the see remained vacant for two years.

Richard Curteys (1570-1583) found the revenues of his see so reduced that he was unable properly to fulfil the ordinary obligations of his position. He did not spare himself in his endeavour to do the duties he had undertaken. With the assistance of others he methodically instructed the diocese under his charge, and so well was this done that a contemporary said "the people with ardent zeale, wonderful rejoicinge, and in great number, take farre and long journeys to be partakers of his good and godly lessons."[38] This excellent man, however, owing to the political spoliation of the church, died impoverished in 1583.

From 1583 till 1585 no bishop was appointed, but in the latter year **Thomas Bickley** (1585-1596) was selected.

Antony Watson (1596-1605) was Bishop of Chichester when James became king. He was occupied much in furthering Whitgift's endeavour to improve the condition of the Church in England by urging conformity to the newly ordered methods of ecclesiastical government and procedure.

Launcelot Andrews (1605-1609) then ruled the diocese until he was transferred to Ely.

He was followed by **Samuel Harsnett** (1609-1619), who was an opponent of the Calvinistic attitude of thought. The records of his visitations ask some pertinent questions, which show how the Cathedral Church itself was being served. He inquires, "Have not many of the vicars and lay vicars been absent for months together? Is the choir sufficiently furnished, and are the boys properly instructed? What has become of the copes and vestments? Who is responsible for the custody of them and of the books? Are there not ale-houses in the close? Why are all these things not amended since the last visitation?" This was the state of affairs in the cathedral church of the diocese at the beginning of the seventeenth century; and during the two hundred years that followed there is but little improvement to remark. Certainly in **George Carleton**'s (1619-1628) and in **Richard Montagu**'s day (1628-1638) there was not much change, for the latter asks in every parish "whether communicants 'meekly kneel,' or whether they stand or sit at the time of reception: Whether the Holy Table is profaned at any time by persons sitting upon it, casting hats or cloaks upon it, writing or casting up accounts or any other

---

[38] Kennett's Notes: see Stephens' "Diocesan History of Chichester," p. 197.

indecent usuage."[39] And in consequence the archbishop desired to restore some sense of order and decency to the minds of both the clergy and laity by replacing the altars in their proper positions again. He asks, therefore, Bishop **Brian Duppa** (1638-1641), in the questions put during the first visitation of parish churches, "Is your communion-table, or altar, strong, fair and decent? Is it set according to the practice of the ancient Church, — upon an ascent at the east end of the chancel, with the ends of it north and south? Is it compassed in with a handsome rail to keep it from profanation according to an order made in the metropolical visitation?"[40]

During the episcopate of **Henry King** (1642-1670) the diocese was a theatre of rebellion and civil war. Chichester was taken on December 29th, 1642, by Waller and the Parliamentary soldiers after a siege of eight days. Bishop King repaired, after the Restoration, the wrecked cathedral and the episcopal palace, but this appears to be all that is known of him.

Peter Gunning (1670-1675) was the first Bishop of Chichester appointed after the Restoration. He had suffered for the tenacity with which he clung to his principles during the period of the Rebellion. Having been ejected from a fellowship at Cambridge, he came to London, and there, with no little audacity, he ministered and taught as a loyalist and Churchman.

But **Ralph Brideoake** (1675-1678) watched the political and ecclesiastical weathercocks, and feathered his nest. He had been "Chaplain to Speaker Lenthall, who gave him the rich living of Witney, near Oxford, where we are told he 'preached twice every Lord's Day, and in the evening catechised the youth in his own house; outvying in labour and vigilancy any of the godly brethren in those parts.' In 1659 he was made one of the 'triers,' yet immediately after the Restoration he was rapidly promoted to a canonry at Windsor, to the Deanery of Salisbury, and finally to the Bishopric of Chichester."[41] Though Bishop Henry King had endeavoured to restore the cathedral and the buildings of the precincts, these still were in a state of extreme dilapidation, for Bishop Brideoake's record of his visitation shows that the towers, windows, and cloisters had not yet been repaired.

Guy Carleton (1678-1685) was a Royalist bishop of a most consistent type. On two occasions he had been turned out of a cure by the Parliamentary "triers" for his opinions; but in his eighty-second year he came from the see of Bristol to Chichester.

Another Royalist, who as a soldier had supported the cause of Charles I., occupied the see after Carleton. This was **John Lake** (1685-1689). He was one of those seven bishops who protested against James's Declaration of Indulgence.

Simon Patrick (1689), **Robert Grove** (1691), **John Williams** (1696), **Thomas Manningham** (1709), **Thomas Bowers** (1722), and **Edward Waddington** (1724) served in the episcopate successively.

Francis Hare (1731-1740) then filled the vacancy. He wasted some of his time

---

[39] Stephens' "Diocesan History," p. 216.
[40] Quoted by Stephens, "Diocesan History," p. 216.
[41] Stephens' "Diocesan History," p. 233.

in useless controversy, and, as the Duke of Marlborough's chaplain, made his office cheap, though perhaps popular, by occasionally dilating in his sermons upon the genius and military skill of his patron. He was a man of some capacity, who advised conformity to the meagre and starved ideals of the then accepted orthodoxy. Apparently he deemed this course a safe one, where there could, it appears, be little other guidance for those who still had any faith, except in the conventionalities of what had become ecclesiastical custom. He saw that the interpretation which individual opinion in its practical rejection of Christian ordinances would read into faith was likely to be no more than a new expression of early and mediæval heresies.

Mathias Mawson (1740-1754) was bishop after Hare; and then Sir **William Ashburnham** (1754-1799) came to the diocese and occupied the see for forty-five years, "the longest episcopate since the foundation of the see."[42]

Before the close of the eighteenth century **John Buckner** (1799-1824) succeeded Ashburnham.

In 1824 **Robert James Carr**, and in 1831 **Edward Maltby**, were appointed to the see.

William Otter succeeded (1836-1840). During his episcopate the Diocesan Association was founded in 1838 to help the clergy and laity of the diocese to provide themselves with better schools, to increase the means of instruction and ministration, to restore or enlarge their churches and schools, and to provide new ones when they had the opportunity afforded by sufficient means. Bishop Otter and Dean Chandler succeeded in establishing a theological college in the city.

Philip N. Shuttleworth (1840-1842), **Ashurst Turner Gilbert** (1842-1870), and **Richard Durnford** (1870-1895) were succeeded by **Ernest Roland Wilberforce**, the present bishop, who was translated to the see from Newcastle in 1895.

---

[42] *Stephens, p, 245.*

S. B. Bolas & Co., photo.

S. CLEMENT'S CHAPEL, AND TOMB OF BISHOP DURNFORD.

DEANS OF CHICHESTER.

Odo, 1115.

Richard, 1115.

Matthew, 1125.

Richard, 1144.

William Fleshmonger, 1526.

Richard Camden, 1541.

Giles Eyre, S.T.D, 1549.

Bartholomew Traheron, S.T.P., 1551-1552.

John de Greneford, 1150.

Jordan de Meleburn, 1176.

Seffride, 1178.

Matthew de Chichester, 1180.

Nicholas de Aquila, 1190.

Seffride, 1197.

Simon de Perigord, 1220.

Walter, 1230.

Thomas de Lichfield, 1232.

Geoffrey, 1250.

Walter de Glocestrin, 1256.

William de Brakelsham, 1276.

Thomas de Berghstede, 1296.

William de Grenefeld, 1302.

John de St. Leophardo, 1307.

Henry de Garland, 1332.

Walter de Segrave, 1342.

William de Lenne, 1356.

Roger de Freton, 1369.

Richard le Scrope, 1383.

William de Lullyngton, 1389-1390.

John de Maydenhith, 1400.

John Haselee, 1407.

Henry Lovel, 1410.

Richard Talbot, 1415.

William Milton, 1420.

John Patten, or Waynflete, 1425.

John Crutchere, 1429.

John Waynfleet, 1478.

John Gloos, 1481.

John Prychard, 1501.

Geoffrey Symson, 1504.

John Young (Bishop), S.T.P. 1508.

Thomas Sampson, S.T.P., 1552-1553.

William Pye, 1553.

Hugh Turnbull, 1558.

Richard Curteis, 1566.

Anthony Rushe, 1570.

Martin Culpepper, M.D, 1577.

William Thome, 1601.

Francis Dee, 1630.

Richard Steward, 1634-1635.

Bruno Ryves, 1646.

Joseph Henshaw, 1660.

Joseph Gulston, S.T.P., 1663.

Nathaniel, Lord Crew, LL.D., 1669.

Thomas Lambrook, 1671.

George Stradling, S.T.P., 1672.

Francis Hawkins, S.T.P.,1688.

William Hayley, S.T.P., 1699.

Thomas Sherlock, 1715.

John Newey, 1727.

Thomas Hayley, D.D., 1735-1736.

James Hargraves, D.D., 1739.

William Ashburnham, Bart., 1741.

Thomas Ball, A.M., 1754.

Charles Harward, 1770.

Combe Miller, 1790.

Christopher Bethell, 1814.

Samuel Slade, 1824.

George Chandler, D.C.L., 1830.

Walter Farquhar Hook, D.D., 1859.

John William Burgon, D.D., 1875.

Francis Pigou, D.D., 1887.

Richard William Randall, D.D., 1892.

BISHOPS OF SELSEA AFTER EADBERT.

Eolla, 714.

Bernege, or Beornegus, 909-922.

Sigga, or Sigfrid, 733.

Aluberht, 739.

Osa, or Bosa, 765-770.

Gislehere, 780.

Totta, 785.

Wiohtun, or Peletun, 789-805.

Aethelwulf, 811-816.

Cenred, 824-838.

Gutheard, 860-862.

Aelfred, 931-940.

Aethelgar, 944-953.

Ordbright, 963-979.

Ealmar, 944-953.

Aethelric I., 1032-1038.

Hecca, 1047-1057.

Aethelric II, 1058-1070.

Stigand, 1070.

ANCIENT BUILDINGS IN THE CITY.

Amongst other interesting architectural monuments, closely connected with the cathedral or the bishops, the following may be particularly noticed:

The **Bishop's Palace** has an interesting chapel, in which a small fresco of the "Virgin and Child" of an early date is still preserved. The dining-room has a panelled wooden ceiling. The painting on it was originally executed in Sherborne's day, but it has suffered by decay and attempts at restoration since the sixteenth century.

The **Vicars' Hall** is to the south-east of the cathedral.

The **Canon Gate** is the archway in South Street, which leads to the palace, the deanery, and other buildings connected with the cathedral.

The **Market Cross** was built by Bishop Storey about the year 1500 (see illustration, p. 100).

S. Mary's Hospital was founded about the middle of the twelfth century; but the existing building dates from the end of the thirteenth century. It maintains five aged women by a weekly allowance to each, with fuel and medical attendance free.

PAINTED DECORATION FORMERLY ON THE CHOIR VAULT,
FROM AN ENGRAVING BY T. KING, 1814.

(Lent by the Reverend Prebendary Bennett.)
(Scale about 7 feet 10½ inches to 1 inch.)

DIMENSIONS.

Length (extreme)	*internal*	393 feet.
Length of nave	*internal*	155 feet.
Width of nave (extreme)	*internal*	90 feet.
Length of choir	*internal*	115 feet.
Length of transept	*internal*	131 feet.
Width of transept	*internal*	33 feet.
Height of vault	*internal*	61 feet.
Height of spire	*internal*	277 feet.
Area		28,000 sq. feet.

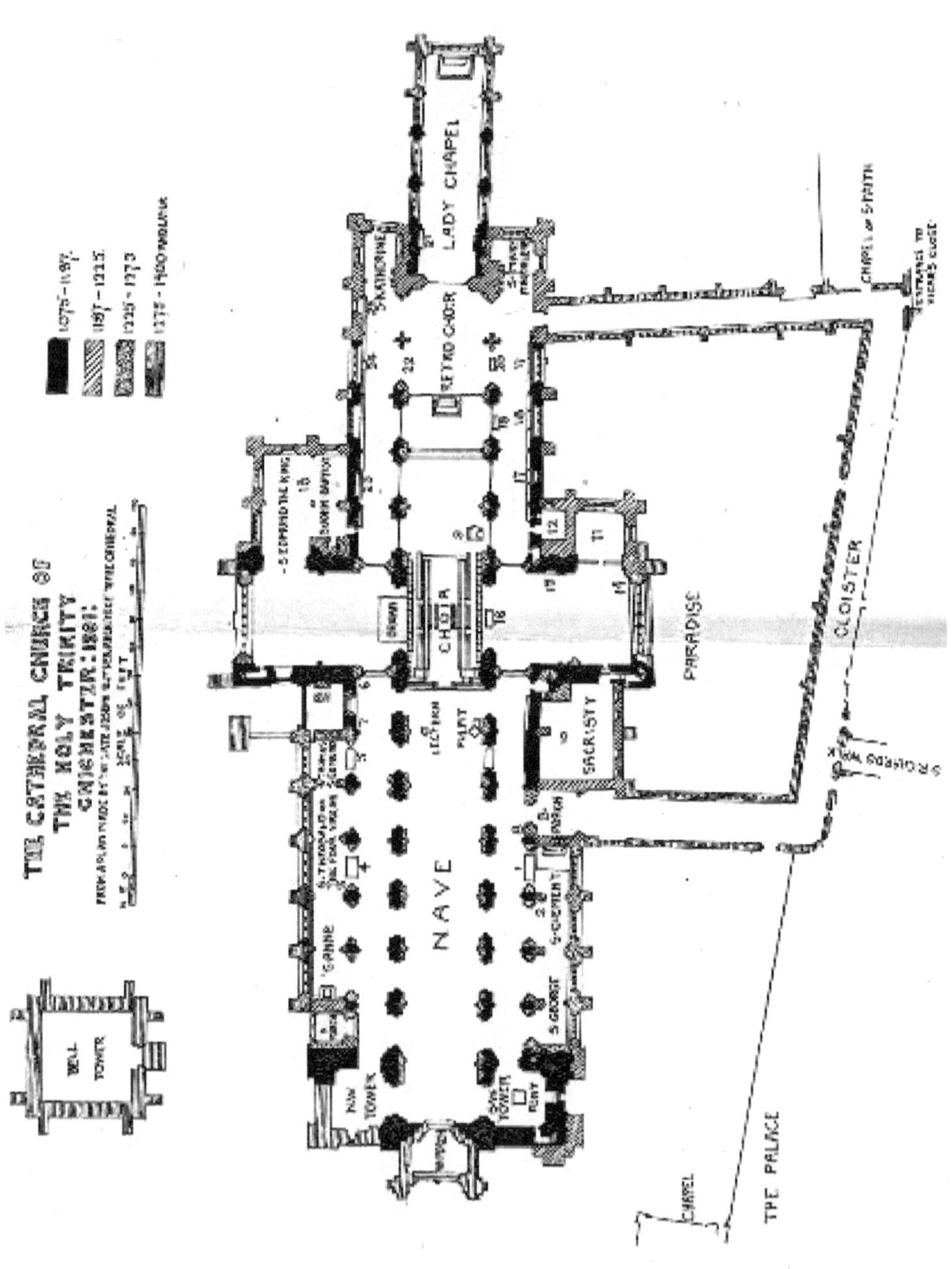

PLAN OF THE CATHEDRAL CHRUCH OF THE HOLY TRINITY
CHICHESTER (1901).

INDEX.

Lector House believes that a society develops through a two-fold approach of continuous learning and adaptation, which is derived from the study of classic literary works spread across the historic timeline of literature records. Therefore, we aim at reviving, repairing and redeveloping all those inaccessible or damaged but historically as well as culturally important literature across subjects so that the future generations may have an opportunity to study and learn from past works to embark upon a journey of creating a better future.

This book is a result of an effort made by Lector House towards making a contribution to the preservation and repair of original ancient works which might hold historical significance to the approach of continuous learning across subjects.

HAPPY READING & LEARNING!

LECTOR HOUSE LLP
E-MAIL: lectorpublishing@gmail.com